A Gnost Progress:
Magic and the Path of Awakening

by Steve Dee

The Universe Machine

A Gnostic's Progress ©2016 Steve Dee

ISBN 978-0-9954904-1-3

All rights reserved. No part of this publication may be reproduced or transmitted in any form or by any means, electronic or mechanical, including photocopying, recording or by any information retrieval system without the prior written permission of the copyright owner, except for brief quotations in a review.

Original artwork: ©2014 & 2015 Lloyd Keane

(All other images are commons licensed.)

Editing, typesetting, and design: Nikki Wyrd

First published in May, 2016 by The Universe Machine, Norwich.

Dedication:

Lots of love and thank yous to Jo, Adam and Melissa.

Many Thanks to Lyn, Julian and Nikki for sharing the zen-gnostic explorations.

Big thanks to Andrew, Miguel and Lainie for the encouragement and to Lloyd for a great interview and some brilliantly weird art.

Steve Dee, March 2016

Contents

Foreword

From the fragments of biography given in this book we should conclude that Steve Dee is a weird and fucked-up guy. At the age of 14 he became a born-again Christian. Then he began training as an Anglican priest. He had uncertainties about his sexuality. He had a breakdown. He now has an altar in his house in Devon with gods on it. He is involved in a magical movement that is best known for the technique of wanking to homemade sigils and using cartoon characters instead of gods. Yet he comes over as very sane.

It is this combination that I particularly like in Steve's work. I haven't yet met him, but I sense he is the guy you can have a drink with in a pub who shares every out-there, marginal—no, liminal—interest that you have. He is less fidgety than you, less argumentative, more laidback. He can talk easily on all sorts of subjects. But when you speak he listens. This is what comes over in these short essays. Although he has a pinch of salt for every out-there idea and a joke for every wayward esoteric author, you sense that he has not just read what they write, but he has listened.

His day job is that of a psychotherapist, and I assume that his clients respond well to him. He would have made a lovely vicar, but the narrowness of church dogma would have ruined him, or at least straitjacketed him for a while. If he had worn the dog collar, one imagines that he would have exploded out of the role during a mid-life crisis, earning column inches in the Daily Mail as some journalist describes the Welsh vicar in a quiet Devon parish who suddenly started taking mind-expanding drugs and placed statues of the Buddha and Baphomet in the village church.

Steve Dee's combination of Chaos magic, Gurdjieff and Gnosticism is fairly close to my own core spiritual approach. Perhaps the difference between us is in practical application. The Gurdjieff work (or a version of it) and, more recently magic, remain the most practical part of my spirituality, apart from spontaneous visits of attention and self-remembering and strangeness. Gnosticism itself, although it has been in one form or other the centre of my writings, has been more a process of research and historical understanding. It hasn't informed my worldview in a central way, except occasionally as experiment. Perhaps I should indicate that here I am speaking of the kind of Gnosticism as represented in the Nag Hammadi Library, not the broader concept of Gnosis as the experiential side of religion and spirituality. Steve, on the other hand, is demonstrably eager to *do something* with Gnosticism. Anyone who feels the same way will find plenty of examples of devotional and magical approaches to the legacy of the Gnostics here.

These essays may be delivered in bite-sized chunks but these are nourishing savouries not quick-fix sugar bombs. He is very aware of being a modern or postmodern spiritual explorer: "We make no claims to lineage or secrets shared on Grandma's knee,

8

rather this is a Witchcraft born of a connection to a raw coastline, the beating of drums and a desire to awaken."

So enter a world filled with speedo-clad yogis and surfer fundamentalists, in which the ancient Nag Hammadi text *Thunder Perfect Mind* is declaimed to a backdrop of trance drumming. Steve's writings do not merely reflect a lowest common denominator of the above influences, a Venn diagram intersection of three or four contemporary spiritual trends. His tastes are more eclectic than that, perhaps, but more importantly I sense that he is always bringing his experience to bear and is always trying things out. As the reader will discover, Steve even encourages us to try things out too.

Andrew Phillip Smith

Editor of *The Gnostic: A Journal of Gnosticism, Western Esotericism and Spirituality.*

Setting Out...

Safe here on the shore, the sand is firm beneath your feet and the sun provides your bones with a reassuring heat. It's safe here, but you know it's time to go. For years you've paddled, frolicked and splashed in the warmth of the shallows and yet the ocean beckons you. While the dark, cold depths fill you with dread, the mystery calls to you. This is about risk and this is about possibility: the chance to loosen our grip on the familiar and to take hold of something yet unseen.

Our boat is waiting, now is the time to head out into deep water to seek the knowledge only experience brings.

Gnostic

Beginnings

I was always a bit of a strange child. In the midst of my family moving to the other side of the planet, I was busy beginning a journey into the depths of my internal world.

Introvert can often have a sense of the pejorative, but when used in its Jungian sense (making sense of the external world by starting from the internal) it's probably a fair descriptor. While I don't view my childhood sensitivity as being that exceptional, I was aware that my desire to understand and map out my sense of self was of real importance to me.

Due to my Mum bravely enduring some pre-natal yoga, we had a couple of volumes in our small book collection. I can clearly recollect the bemused looks my Dad gave me as I valiantly sought to recreate the black and white images of the speedo-clad yogis. However faltering these attempts may have been, I was intoxicated by the idea that I could use my body and movement as a means for exploring who I was. While concepts like faith and belief were quite foreign to me, having not come from a religious family, I was able to connect to the idea that there were physical practices for navigating this strange inner terrain.

My family had moved to the Gold Coast in the Australian state of Queensland. For those not familiar with it, the Gold

Coast (at least in the late 70s and early 80s) was a mecca of surfing, the hotel industry and the edges of a diverse spiritual and musical sub-culture. For the adolescent me, my early meditative forays found an outlet via a number of yoga centres and Hare Krishna restaurants. Though I was probably too young to be seen as a serious aspirant, people were kind and allowed me to amass piles of free literature. While my working-class family were undoubtedly bemused/ horrified by some of the religious and dietary experiments that I was pursuing, I am deeply grateful for the tolerance that they demonstrated as I sought to forge my way.

Confessions of a Teenage Evangelical...

At the same time as I began to experiment with yoga and meditation practice at about the age of 10, I had also begun meeting people who wouldn't stop talking about Jesus. While I was regularly chanting mantras and performing sun salutations, I also kept bumping into some fairly wide-eyed Christian surfers who were keen to tell me that I was a sinner worshipping false Gods!

The psychoanalyst Erik Erikson has highlighted that teenage years can be a confusing time as we seek to navigate the core dilemma of "identity formation vs. confusion". For the fourteen-year-old version of Steve Dee, the confusion about both my sexuality and spiritual identity were worrying enough that I felt in need of rescuing from myself. This rescue came in the form of "going forward" at an evangelistic rally and "accepting Jesus as my personal friend and saviour." Although I was consistently unconvinced about their claims of exclusive truth, the lure of forgiveness and the sense of belonging that this form of church had on offer were enough to bring me into the fold.

Looking back, I can see that during those early years as a believer I was definitely in a child-like state, in wanting to be fed certainties that would calm the turmoil that I was feeling. My faith undoubtedly did this for me, but as I was to learn, the suppression of core drives and central aspects of the self rarely come without serious consequences:

> *"If you bring forth what is within you, what you bring forth will save you. If you do not bring forth what is within you, what you do not bring forth will destroy you."*

The Gospel of Thomas

The payback that I eventually experienced came during an under-graduate degree in theology at a conservative seminary a few years after my family had returned to the UK. As my certainty was replaced with confusion, anxiety and eventual hallucinations, my psyche began to give way. It's fair to say that the process was far from pretty, but the fact that I'm writing this evidences the efficacy of prodigious amounts of tea drinking, with friends who weren't in a hurry to respond to my demands for exorcism! In addition to the healing power of community I was also greatly aided by the stillness of contemplative prayer and a growing interest in psychological therapies.

My time at college was a truly heady experience that I still feel was of great value. In the midst of my own emotional turmoil, I was asked to dig into topics as diverse as the early Church Fathers and the work of that great wizard Carl Gustav Jung.

In trying to make sense of Jung's hugely innovative exploration of concepts, such as the shadow and the collective unconscious, I felt as though I had found a role model who gave me permission to reconnect to my own creativity. Via my attempts at trying to understand Jung's contribution to Western psychology, I learnt not only about his role in safe-guarding a part of the valuable Nag Hammadi library, but also the parallels between his depth psychology and the Gnostic's emphasis on self-liberation.

From a personal perspective I needed to re-access those aspects of my identity that I had pushed underground. I needed to embrace my sense of fey, liminal Queerness, and to embrace the playful curiosity that my attempt at orthodoxy had clamped down on.

In contrast to a faith-based approach to belief, Jung's contemporary re-visioning of Western alchemical traditions made vivid the idea that the making of Soul was something that we could consciously cultivate. For the conscious explorer of this territory, the application of art, dreaming and active reflection can become magical tools. While my own crisis of faith had ultimately derailed my initial plan of becoming an Anglican Priest, it did make me keenly aware of a hunger to discover these means for myself.

> "*Your vision will become clear only when you can look into your own heart. Who looks outside, dreams; who looks inside, awakes.*"
>
> *Carl Jung*

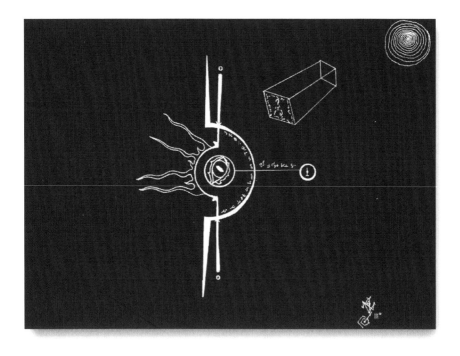

Black Horizons

Progress

Strange Revelations

It's hardly surprising that more mainstream Christians of the second century found the Gnostics troubling – while outwardly appearing orthodox in many ways, with their vivid and at times anarchic mythologies, their take on the nature of the divine was radically subversive.

For the religious philosopher the knotty issue of theodicy (the problem of evil) has always proven to be of a decidedly Gordian nature. Whether our gods are singular or plural, if we attach to them either omnipotence or omniscience then the reality of human pain is likely to raise some awkward questions regarding their goodness.

In wrestling with this dilemma, the solution that the Gnostics proposed was highly avant garde. For the majority of the Gnostics, the realm of nature and the God of the Old Testament were incompatible with the picture of the divine painted by Christ in the New Testament. If both Yahweh and the natural world were capricious and violent, how could one reconcile this with the 'heavenly Father' that Jesus believed was ever listening and attentive? For many Gnostics, the tribal, desert God of the old covenant represented at best an outdated perception of the

Pleroma's true nature; at worst this 'God' was a deceiver actively seeking to blind humanity to the divine spark within.

While recently revisiting some of the Gnostic's primary sources in June Singer's excellent *A Gnostic Book of Hours*, I was once again struck by the novelty of their solution to our experience of suffering:

> *Yaldabaoth (the demiurge) stole power from his mother (Sophia), for he was ignorant,*
> *Thinking there existed no other except his mother alone...*
> *When the Arrogant One saw the creation which surrounds him*
> *And the multitude of angels which had come forth from him,*
> *He exalted himself above these and said to them:*
> *"I am a jealous God, and there is no God besides me."*

The Apocryphon of John

When we attempt to engage with its primary texts we see a complexity and variation that mustn't be minimised in an attempt to homogenise the subtle variety of narratives regarding our beginnings. While many present day magical practitioners may reference "gnosis" as an experiential short-hand for the in-coming of new insights, many scholars of early Gnosticism would be keen to place an emphasis on cosmic dualism as being one of the defining characteristics of those traditions that they are seeking to categorise.

Unsuprisingly much ink has been spilt debating the merits of various historic groups and schools and whether they can truly be categorised as Gnostic. Some wish to use the descriptor only

18

in relation to those holding a more radical dualism like the Sethians (cf. Brakke 2010), while many also want to include traditions like the Valentinians, who held the somewhat gentler view that the imperfection of matter was due to the dilution of the divine essence within it. Whichever position one holds, I think that we can maintain that both groups felt the need to evolve unorthodox cosmologies in order to make sense of the world.

The shape of the cosmic myths that these groups employed were invariably complex, creative and somewhat fluid in the roles that this mythic cast played on the Cosmic stage:

The Cast

The Pleroma: The perfect original divine state. A Primary unmoved unity that is ultimately beyond direct approach and description.

Sophia: Divine Wisdom (often depicted as feminine), who in acting out of independence or pride separates herself from the Pleroma and in some sense "falls" into a lower state.

The Demiurge: The result of Sophia's creative activity is the production of a lesser being or demiurge, who then either creates the material world or takes credit for having created it. The Gnostics often viewed this lesser god as being synonymous with the God of the Old Testament and the false-authority to which the uninitiated paid homage.

Aeons and Archons: Gnostic cosmologies were generally populated by a whole host of beings who could be called upon to either assist us (Aeons) or could be experienced as hindering our spiritual progress (Archons). Part of the challenge for the intrepid explorer was trying to work out which ones were which.

In many ways the radical dualism of many Gnostic schools is hardly surprising given their life expectancy, infant mortality and the lack of decent dental care! While I might struggle with such perspectives, I'm also aware that my own somewhat rose-tinted eco-consciousness may largely be based on my own Western privilege and the current availability of antibiotics.

While an acknowledgement of such a dualistic perspective may be critical in ensuring that my own understanding of Gnosticism had a solid historical foundation, I am still aware of my personal ambivalence towards such perspectives. As much as I may take inspiration from the creative individualism of much Gnostic material, I have to remain honest about my own questions and discomfort regarding the psychological and environmental wisdom of holding such a worldview.

While such tensions are very real, it is also important that we consider them within the context of the radical hermeneutic that they brought to their engagement with story and scripture. Given that the Gnostics appeared to have placed a far higher value on a more experiential and non-historic approach to the Christ story, one might question the degree to which they themselves viewed such cosmological models literally. Yes, they would have had significant philosophical and theological messages to convey, but they were also profoundly concerned with seeking liberation and using story in order to trigger direct experience.

In seeking to wrestle with the radicalism of early Gnostic dualism, many contemporary revivalists of the tradition have sought to evolve a more nuanced position by emphasising the similarities between the gnostic message and the central dilemmas faced in both Buddhist and Existentialist philosophies (Hoeller 2002). The core concerns of both these world-views regarding dissatisfaction and impermanence, have considerable overlap with the Gnostic's longing for both salvation and significance that are not defined by the apparent fragility of the material realm. Later in the book we'll spend some time considering the degree to which Buddhist, Existential and Gnostic perspectives intersect with each other, especially as we try to think about what a contemporary Gnostic practice might look like.

The Joy of Process Theology

My book shelves are groaning under the weight of books about Gnosticism! Since the discovery in 1945 of the texts that we now classify as the Nag Hammadi Library, there has been an explosion of interest in the history of Gnosticism and how these groups interacted with the wider Christian community.

During my time at theological college I became deeply fascinated by Church history. While many of my fellow-students viewed it as being a somewhat dusty and tedious subject, I was fascinated by these clerical detective stories and the vital importance that various councils and synods had in shaping the human experience of belief.

However enthralling this material might be, many able thinkers have already spilt considerable amounts of ink considering the timeline of historic Gnosticism. What I'm interested in exploring is whether the Gnostics can be viewed as more than a museum piece and whether their insights have continued relevance as we try to explore ideas around awakening, enlightenment, and what it might mean to be human in the 21st century.

In seeking to understand how the Gnostic experience might intersect with my own, I am all too aware of the danger of projecting onto them my own personal and spiritual agendas. As I struggle to locate historic role models that might exemplify my own desire for liberty, I'm aware that I might overly focus on the

Gnostics as some sort of existential freedom fighters and that in doing so, I might be minimising their potentially hostile view of the material world. Of course none of us come to this (or any other) material without our own presuppositions and biases, and I think it's only fair to acknowledge my own as both an aspiring Process theologian and a creative magical practitioner.

For the uninitiated, Process Theology is deeply interested in what the emergence of religious myth reveals about the shape and concerns of human consciousness. Even a cursory study of religious phenomena reveals both our greatest aspirations and the depths of our prejudices. Inspired by Theologians such as A.N. Whitehead and John Cobb, Process Theology sees our understanding of the numinous realm as being part of an unfolding story that is profoundly influenced by our human experience of life. Revelation or the incoming of new religious information comes both within a human context and also always in response to it, as Whitehead states "God grows with the world, always in process" (1967). Humanity's religious expressions, be they tribal deities, anthropomorphized monotheisms, or Lovecraftian terrors, all mirror our collective journey through history.

To see value in the insights of Process Theology is not to imply some removal of mystery; rather it glories in religion as an art. Advocates of this approach of course differ as to the extent to which our gods are created by us. Some may believe that the core being of God is objectively out there and it is primarily our perception that is evolving; others more radically may feel that the gods are real precisely because we've made them so (see Terry Pratchett's *Small Gods* for a fantastic exposition on this approach).

One fine example of Process Theology in action are the differing views that the Gnostic schools had on the role and identity of the Demiurge. While the radical Sethian dualists tended to view Ialdabaoth as a blind idiot god full of pride and self-deception, others were not so harsh. For the Valentinians who seemed more interested in remaining part of orthodox Christianity, the Demiurge took on a somewhat softer Neoplatonic hue. Rather than being an agent of the devil, he was the victim of his own distance from the Godhead. For those who embrace this perspective, as the divine essence descends into matter it is inevitable that it becomes more dilute and thus prone to imperfection.

As I sought to dig into the Gnostic material, my own hunch was that the Demiurge gets a bit of a hard time and ends up becoming some sort of cosmic whipping boy. In most Gnostic myths, while the Pleroma takes things easy as the "unmoved mover" in some sort of idealised heavenly chill-out zone, it's the feisty Sophia and her wayward son who actually get on with doing something! Good ideas are great, but unless they work their way through to planning and creative expression, they remain ideas only. The Demiurge arguably represents the messy reality of how we produce and maintain a creative endeavor. As humans we may long for an idealised state in which nothing dies and pain never gets felt, but our shared experience of what happens day-to-day is far from this. Our yearning for Platonic ideals and the Perfect may well be part of our evolving consciousness, but it may be that the complex joy and chaos of Life is like this because it couldn't function otherwise.

In trying to appreciate these potent myths, I found myself reflecting on part of my day job as a Systemic psychotherapist. Unlike more traditional forms of psychotherapy that tend to focus on a deeper truth located within the individual, Systemic therapy seeks to explore the dynamics and meaning that is created *between* members of a system.

Many recent writers on Gnosticism have been keen to emphasise the parallels between its myths, and the insights of Jungian depth psychology (Hoeller 1982 and Singer 1992). While I generally find great value in such reflections, I would question whether the Jungian emphasis on the individual has sidelined the insights that can also be gained in trying to appreciate the relationships that exist between the mythic figures on this cosmic stage.

In seeking to grapple with the dynamics at play within Gnostic cosmology it didn't feel that dissimilar to the issues that arise as I work with Families (of all shapes and sizes) in the therapy room. In one corner we have the Pleroma as the somewhat distant father figure, seemingly critical of his wayward son's attempts to make his way in the multiverse ("Dad you just don't understand! I just want to create and make stuff happen!"). In the middle of this conflict we have a somewhat care-worn Sophia trying to mediate between these two. It's not easy being caught in the middle between a numinous perfection you respect and a wayward but creative rebel you don't want to lose!

Making sense of Gnosticism is never easy, even with these reflections, we still need to engage with the core dilemma of how we seek to reconcile our ever-changing, messy world with this very human longing for greater stillness and a tranquil, more reliable numinous realm.

In seeking to actively engage with the dualism present in the primary texts of the Gnostics it would be easy to problematize the tensions that exist in the dynamics between the Pleroma, Sophia and the Demiurge. In contrast to this perspective, I find myself being curious about the manner in which they may be viewed as encapsulating the core process of how we as humans wrestle with dilemmas, of both our humanity and creativity. The threefold schema of hylic, psychic and pneumatic (approximately body, soul and spirit) reflects the dynamic tension that many of us experience in our lives. Those of us drawn to engaging with the Gnostic material are usually well aware of these dilemmas, and are rarely placated by either simple answers or promises of peace.

In trying to manage this apparent dialectic we are continually at risk of going into denial about either part of this equation by burying ourselves in either materialist reductionism on one hand or spiritual fantasy on the other. The trickier and more challenging alternative that we will explore is how we might work with the dynamic tension that is an intrinsic part of this polarity. By employing the perspectives of both Systemic therapy and Process Theology, we can potentially gain new insights as to how the unfolding relationships between these figures mirror our own attempts to make sense of both ourselves and the world around us.

Key to managing this tension is the role of Sophia, the embodiment of divine wisdom. We need to return to the wisdom of the Mother. Between Pleroma and Demiurge lies Sophia and although some of the gnostic myths want to lay blame at her door for seeking independence, Sophia seems to be key in understanding how the realm of the ideal works alongside our experience of reality. Wisdom (that heady fusion of intellect, experience and intuition) allows us to oil the cogs in helping our ideas become plans, our plans become actions and our actions become Art.

Dancing with the Demiurge

Whether the act of creation is viewed as rebellion against the Pleroma or an inevitable and necessary process, the status of the Demiurge as a lesser God of most Gnostic mythology seems to imply that matter is at best imperfect, and at worst a realm of hell that they needed to escape from. As we have already considered, the Gnostics were grappling with the dilemma of living in a world where impermanence and human suffering were all too apparent.

While the more radically dualistic forms of Gnosticism may view the Demiurge as being the enemy of those seeking to awaken, I personally feel that for the contemporary explorer, a more complex relationship can be evolved. For me, the variety of ways in which the Demiurge can be viewed, reflects some of the key dynamics and dilemmas present for those of us trying to understand the present day relevance of the Gnostic message.

The Demiurge can help us realize the inescapable limitations in our human efforts to describe the numinous realm. All attempts at trying to imagine the divine realm are limited when we seek to use positive statements and language to describe it. When faced with both our finite perception (even when under mystical inspiration) and our descriptive limitations, it is hard to escape the realisation that these are "fingers pointing at the moon". Out of necessity we end up with a negative or apophatic theology of God i.e. described as not being like this and not being like that. However helpful a divine revelation at a given point in time, we must face that it will become outdated as our perception shifts and evolves. Such visions can become Demiurgical husks that prevent our openness to incoming insight if we fail to grasp their temporal nature.

An acknowledgement of the limitations inherent in even the most skillful religious metaphor can be deeply liberating. Whilst past perceptions of the divine can function as little more that outdated conventions, they can become more pernicious if they prevent our individual or collective growth. While these great images and stories can provide invaluable insights into how our consciousness has tried to deal with reality, they can so easily become limiting clutter. Like constraining Archons, these dusty modalities can hold back our attempts to forge new understanding and ways to interact with our world.

While our religious projects will always be at risk of entropy and decay, it is possible to see the Gnostic drama as a dance between the principles of flux and permanence. The stillness and unchanging perfection of the Pleroma may appear to contrast with the fluctuating realm of matter, but when we consider the apparent scarcity of life in the known universe, perhaps it can only exist according to the principles of change and evolution that we currently experience. Life (as we can perceive it) is as it is, because it can be no other way.

Rather than viewing the realm of matter and the Demiurge as standing in opposition to the Cosmic reliability of a Godhead, it may be more psychologically viable to view them as interdependent realities within a numinous whole. To some extent, the concept of unfolding ages or Aeons seems to point toward a repeating spiral of conflict, apparent resolution, evolution and new found tension. Rather than becoming overly fixated on a particular divine figure, it may well be possible to explore and discover spiritual meaning in more fully comprehending the relationships and dynamics that might exist **between** figures within a given pantheon. Personally I have found such an approach extremely helpful in my engagement with the unfolding dynamic present within Gnostic Myth.

A number of esoteric groups in recent history have sought to articulate this idea that new understanding might be gained in exploring the systemic dynamics that exist between things, rather than merely within them. Two such groups that are particularly pertinent to our current discussion are the Process Church of the Final Judgment (whom we will consider later) and the Fraternitas Saturni.

The Fraternitas Saturni (or Brotherhood of Saturn) is a magical order founded in Germany in 1928 that developed a unique philosophy that incorporated the law of Thelema with a heady vision of Astrosophy (Planetary focused Gnosis). Time does not permit a lengthy discussion of their beliefs and practices (I would highly recommend Stephen Flowers' work *The*

Fraternitas Saturni), but their insights concerning the role of the Demiurge are highly helpful.

In their complex cosmology, Saturn is both the Demiurge and the guardian of the threshold to true gnosis. Within a solar system where the vision of mundane humanity will focus its eyes sunward, those in pursuit of awakening will seek the darkness of Saturn as a means to balance and depth. Saturn's emphasis on enlightenment, independence and self-control embodies the gnostic goal of *Lux e tenebris*: Light from the Darkness (Flowers pg. 32).

Within the lore of the Fraternitas Saturni (FS), Saturn as demiurge is seen as having both a light and dark aspect that are often described as a "higher" and "lower" octave. While the aspirant must seek to work with both the more visceral, satanic aspects of the lower octave, the overall aim of the initiate is to focus on the higher, Luciferian octave so as to promote independence and to avoid the more unhelpful aspects of the demiurge.

The path of gnostic exploration within the FS is not merely an absorption into the darkness of Saturn, rather it sees the demiurge as a true gateway through which initiatory knowledge can be gained as we seek to balance a whole variety of Stella energies within ourselves.

Waiting at the Event Horizon

Exercise 1: Sculpting Your System

One of the techniques that I often employ during my own Systemic psychotherapy practice is that of the Sculpt. Sculpting is a tool for making an external picture or sculpt of an internal process such as feelings, experiences, or perceptions. It can use features such as body posture and spacing as demonstrations of relationship patterns, where these relate to communication, power, closeness, and distance. Sculpts can take many forms, they can involve the placement of individuals in proximity to each in order to capture something of their relationship with each other e.g. "You've chose to stand behind your son, does that mean that you feel protective of him?" or they can utilise objects like buttons or rocks to map out the things that are important to us in our lives. Work with sculpts was pioneered by the brilliant Virginia Satir (see her book *Peoplemaking* 1972); Satir was one of the three therapists of excellence on whose work Richard Bandler and John Grinder based their development of Neuro-Linguistic Programming.

For this exercise I'd like you to find a collection of small objects that you feel can represent the people or interests that are currently important in your life. You might choose something fairly abstract (buttons or rocks) or you might use objects directly connected to a person, e.g. a feather or a chess piece. Make sure you also choose something to represent yourself.

Once you have collected your objects and placed the object representing yourself in the centre of your working space, begin to place these objects in proximity to yourself and each other. Perhaps a sister is currently somewhat distant (she's a smooth black button, very prim and proper), whereas the uncle you've reconnected to (the small toy golf club) is quite close. Don't limit yourself to family or even people. Pets, hobbies, spiritual beliefs, the deceased and your games console can all be represented within your personal universe. Part of the aim of this exercise is to enable us to gain a new appreciation of the elements within our personal universe and to consider whether there are aspects we wish to change.

Often when people use this technique in therapy, the next step is to consider what you might want to move, introduce or remove from the Sculpt. As people move objects closer or further away from each other, the therapist might explore what might need to change for that desire to take hold more objectively. Maybe I need to ring my sister to have that tricky conversation; or if I want those cigarettes out of the picture then I need to get to a chemist. This can be a highly helpful exercise as we think about what might prevent change and also discover things we thought were important but forgot to put in there.

Perhaps it needs stating that this can be a highly poignant undertaking that one should not feel rushed in doing. We are always very conscious within a clinic session of allowing people to disassemble their own sculpts and allowing them to keep a specific object if they feel the need to.

Given that recently we have been thinking about the main players within Gnostic mythology and their inter-relationship, for those of us following an esoteric path it can also be interesting to use a sculpt technique to depict our relationship with our gods, spirits and other spiritual allies. Many magical folk already do this unconsciously via the construction of altars. When we look at these spaces, we can see the way in which we perceive our alliances and also how we want to communicate them to ourselves (and potentially) others. Altars often act as anchor points for our spiritual lives, in which we return to these spaces to reconnect ourselves with the values and worldviews that are important to us during a given time.

Another exercise of potential value is to create a sculpt involving the spiritual forces that one currently sees as being present in your life. You may wish to use small objects again or you may choose to utilise statues and magical tools that are currently integrated within altars or working spaces. When I have done this for myself, I have noted with interest the distance between those things I assumed were important and what I actually found myself putting in my altar/sculpt (in my case there wasn't a chaos star in sight!)

After creating this altar-sculpt, take time to reflect on what its significance might mean for you. Following your reflection you may want to shift, introduce or remove elements of what you have depicted in physical space. The very act of doing this can be an invocatory act as we acknowledge those spiritual realities that we wish to see more present in our lives. As we consider the new map we have created, it can be helpful to make notes of these changes, as these shifts may provide us with directions for further more in-depth ritual work.

My own experience, both therapeutically and in a more ritual context, is that Sculpts can be a highly effective tool for helping us access the less linear aspects of ourselves. They can help promote more visual forms of processing and allow a greater sense of playfulness in that you can't really do it wrong! Anyway, I hope you have fun with it and find it helpful.

Gnosticism as a Liberation Theology

Most religious systems are ultimately designed with the aim of promoting some form of liberation. They may differ in terms of exactly what they think we are in need of liberation from (Sin, Desire, Ignorance, Maya etc.), but my own reading is that they are seeking to offer some sort of solution to our haunting sense of discomfort with our existing cultural structures.

McKnight (1995 ed. Segal) has suggested that a general definition of whether something is Gnostic in nature, relates to the extent that it has "a doctrine of saving knowledge" and while his definition is useful (if somewhat loose), the question remains "salvation or liberation from what?". While it may seem somewhat obvious, it probably bears stating that if Gnosis is liberating knowledge, then it must entail freedom from constrictive ignorance.

In *Europe's Inner Demons*, Norman Cohn masterfully analyses the manner in which the non-conforming and unorthodox were viewed and persecuted as outsiders. One indictment of human nature seems to entail that whether it is Jews, Christians, Gnostics or Witches, if a given group finds itself viewed as being more acceptable, then they tend to vilify any other group who they perceive as threatening their position.

In his analysis of the witch persecutions of the post-Medieval period, Cohn concludes that it was highly unlikely that the fevered imaginings of persecuting clerics had little foundation in

37

reality. What seems more evident is that their actions were overwhelmingly directed at other groups of people who considered themselves Christians. While it is almost inevitable that some of these Christians practised magic (and by doing so, demonstrated their humanity), the fear projected by these clerics was more often motivated by an ungodly desire to control.

The Church's ability to control would always be challenged by the heterodoxy of groups such as the Cathars and the Beguines, in that they not only believed that they had access to spiritual experiences outside of the Church's sacraments, but they also organised themselves outside of their societies' dominant hierarchies. Whatever the degree of adherence might be to such unapproved philosophies by the mainstream of society, the ideas that these outsider groups represented embodied a type of cognitive liberty that eroded the hold of any centralised hegemony.

In the example of the Witch, while we may not buy into Jules Michelet's idealised depiction of the Witch as some sort of satanic freedom fighter, there is something subversive contained within even the simplest act of folk magic. To express a sense of agency through a magical act that uses means outside, or beyond the Church's recognised sacraments, is to commit an act of heteropraxy. Within the collective psyche of Europe, the Witch has often acted as an icon of disturbance and freedom. The projected fantasies of clerics and folkloric imaginings often allude to something dark, disturbing and free. The Witch, the Gnostic and the Heretic become the attractors for the collective projections of a society that needs to move on.

To question orthodoxies and seek new means for personal exploration will inevitably threaten those for whom stability is paramount. Those of us who consciously embrace identities such as "Witch", "Magician" or "Gnostic" are honour bound to aid our own culture in prodding them to embrace diversity, multiplicity and liberty. When we take on this mantle we must remain awake to the reality that we both represent the freedom that so many seek, and that we still risk being scapegoated by those who would seek to control.

Mahayana Gnostics: Part 1

While the beginnings of many religious traditions are decidedly focused on the salvation or liberation of the individual, they rarely remain as such. Given time to evolve and gaze outwards, many religious traditions develop a greater sense of collective responsibility, where the liberation of the individual demands a response to the "other".

The 1950s and 60s witnessed an important movement within the Roman Catholic Church in South America, when people engaged at the coalface of day-to-day hardship re-envisioned the gospel message in relation to political and economic oppression. The Liberation of the Israelites from Egypt, and the Gospel message of Christ, were both viewed as narratives of freedom whereby "the downtrodden were lifted up" (Luke 1:52). With the birth of Liberation Theology in the works of Leonardo Boff, Gustavo Gutierrez et al past dogmas were no longer sufficient, and the rigours of true discipleship were now to be measured in terms of deeds or "praxis". As Desmond Tutu powerfully observed; "If you are neutral in situations of injustice, then you have chosen the side of the oppressor."

In relation to the historical development of a religious tradition such as Buddhism, this shift toward the collective can be seen in the development of the "Greater Vehicle" of the Mahayana tradition. As Kenneth O'Neill highlights in his analysis of the parallels between Buddhist and Gnostic traditions (Segal

1995), the shift towards seeking to assist others embodied in the Bodhisattva vows, contrasts with the Theravadan emphasis on personal attainment of Nirvana. This growth in our awareness of interdependence offers us insight into the possibility that a core part of the healing that we seek for ourselves comes through the offering of service to others.

Exercise 2: The Liberating Journey

In thinking about Liberation Theology we have already touched upon the importance that the Biblical Exodus has as an exemplar of what personal, economic and social freedom might mean. The Exodus is perhaps the central Old Testament of salvation history i.e. the way in which God is seen as intervening in the life of the Jewish people so as to demonstrate his on-going covenant with them.

For the Liberation Theologians the movement from oppression and captivity, through tribulation and wilderness and then on to the Promised Land, provides us with a critical exemplar as to what the Gospel needs to embody. To speak of salvation without there being concrete transformations at a practical grass roots level is to utter empty words.

While the metaphor of a journey is often something of a cliché in spiritual communities, I believe that we can still make effective use of it when applied skilfully. In the case of the Exodus story, rather than it being based on new age meandering, it was a journey that first required a rather stark awakening to the profound discomfort and oppression that the Israelites had been subjected to. Like the Buddha becoming profoundly awakened to the impermanence of the Universe, for us to truly pursue change and transformation we need to view our current dis-ease with open eyes.

If you are considering a journey of change in your own life, you might want to try this exercise that makes use of some insights gleaned from Dialectical Behaviour Therapy (DBT). As is self-evident from its name, this therapy (developed by Marsha Linehan) seeks to use Hegel's thinking on how processes of change occur. DBT looks at how our thinking and emotions can become polarised and cut off from each other. The therapy's goal is focused on developing skills that allow the less connected aspects of ourselves to communicate more effectively.

Step 1. Draw a line down the middle of a blank piece of paper, and on either side draw a circle that has enough space to write inside. Inside of the circle on the left, use words or symbols to describe the current situation that you wish to change. Like the Israelites or the Buddha waking up, we need to view our situation with as much clarity as possible. Some people find it helpful to imagine themselves viewing the situation as if it were occurring to a close friend: what would we feedback to them? How would we describe the nature of the problem or dilemma? What aspect of the situation is most changeable?

Step 2. In the other circle use symbols or words to describe the situation that you wish to journey towards. As you see it in your mind's eye, what things are you doing? Are you wearing specific clothing? What are your surroundings like? These can be vital questions in order to focus your desire to see things change. It will also provide you with a goal (albeit a visualised one) that you can measure your progress against.

Step 3. On another piece of paper re-draw these circles as intersecting like this:

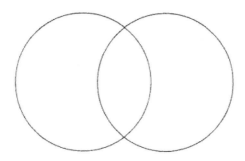

So this is where the rubber hits the road! If we have connected to the situation we are unhappy with and also have a clear vision about where we wish to journey to, how do we use the insights gained to actually begin to make it happen?

The intersection between these two circles is the synthesising point where our desire for freedom needs behavioural expression. In the same way that Liberation Theology places a firm emphasis on praxis, so the behavioural aspect of DBT would insist that we gain the greatest benefit when our longings are translated into actually doing something. The beginnings of this journey will often start with small steps that when they are added together, can cause significant shifts within the eco-system of our current situations.

For example; if we want to ultimately reduce a pattern of habitual/addictive behaviour that we feel is damaging us, how do we start increasing the positive new activity that we want to experience more of? If I want to reduce my smoking in order to improve my yoga practice, I might increase my practice at home or attend a new class so that I can maximise my desire to change the target behaviour (the smoking). By increasing my practice at home I'm reminding myself of why I want to reduce my smoking and by going to a (good) class I'm using the practice of others to reinforce my new activity and to provide myself with inspiration. This then acts as a feedback loop (or spell!) that helps me to reach my ultimate goal i.e. being more healthy.

There are many types of response that can be generated by mapping out change processes in this way. As we let the dialectical tension simmer between what we want and where we currently are, numerous alchemical realities can be generated. We might realise that the change we want is actually something less radical (we might redraw our circles with new goals in mind). Seeing our current situation more clearly may help fuel our motivation and get us reflecting on whom we might invite to join us on this journey (other people's circles begin to intersect with our own).

A psychiatrist once had a sign in their waiting room which read "Either way it hurts". It hurts to change, it hurts if we shy from the challenge and opt for the familiar. To think about change is never without risk, but the alternative of not seeking growth can be a slavery that most Gnostics would struggle to bear.

Hermetic Insights and Gnostic Mood

The discomfort that many of us feel in adopting a radically dualistic attitude toward the world that we know means that many Neo-Gnostics and contemporary practitioners adopt a more a more alchemical view of our origins, which seeks to hold these things together in tension. As we have already highlighted, this more moderate form of "soft" dualism, relies on a more Neoplatonic view of emanation where the reality (and messiness) of life on our planet results from its distance from the original divine source.

This softer perspective certainly allows a greater acknowledgement that we can experience the material world as incredibly beautiful and pleasurable, but within the context of our current discussion we need to consider whether this perspective is truly Gnostic. If we define Gnosticism in the same terms employed by the early Church Fathers in their attacks on heresy, then the answer is almost certainly no. If however we make use of McKnight's looser definition of Gnosis being "a doctrine of saving knowledge" (Segal 1995), then the Hermetic tradition certainly meets that criteria. For me while there seems to be a fairly wide chasm between these two perspectives, I have been left wondering whether there may be a mediating position.

Through the groundbreaking work of Hans Jonas, understandings of historic Gnosticism have been closely linked to the insights of Heidegger and the possible parallels that might exist between the Gnostic worldview and existentialism. While I personally feel that there are great benefits to be gained from Jonas' approach, in my view Heidegger has other keys to offer us as we seek to understand the mood of the Gnostics.

Heidegger recognised that our process of understanding something is a circular, repetitive but progressive act of interpretation. Our "being" in the world is not a sterile state in our heads; rather it is a process of interaction with other people and things. Our connection to the world is not as a result of thought alone; rather it also involves an attunement to mood at both an individual and collective level. This circular process fits well with why it can feel so difficult to understand both historical and contemporary manifestations of the Gnostic current: new information and insights are folded back in on themselves and our ability to capture an ever shifting, evolving entity struggles to escape a certain degree of reductionism.

Certainly within the Corpus Hermeticum we can see something of this unfolding process and mood, as the text itself reflects the tension that exists between on the one hand a radical dualistic, and on the other a softer more Neoplatonic, position. Part of the richness and complexity of the Hermetic tradition is reflected in the fact that the redactors of the current text have incorporated sayings that represent both of these perspectives.

While this may provide the scholar with significant challenges, this is a dynamic tension that runs through the history of many religious traditions. Rather than seeing it as evidence of conflict or contradiction, it may be possible to view such catalyzing tensions as being a critical part of any healthy evolution.

Fans of Hegel's dialectical approach may wonder whether such dialectical tension will inevitably produce a more integrated synthesis, but I would wonder if there is a powerful Gnostic dynamic at work in allowing a less resolved reality. When we arrive at more in-depth discussions around contemporary practice, we will consider whether the jarring strangeness of Gnostic teaching is deliberately designed to generate discomfort, and with discomfort, awakening:

Jesus said, "Those who seek should not stop seeking until they find. When they find, they will be disturbed. When they are disturbed, they will marvel, and will rule over all."

Gospel of Thomas v.2

Contemporary Paths and the Way of the Magician

Any attempt to connect to the mood of Gnosticism will have its own challenges, given both the fragmentary nature of the material and the subjectivity that each of us brings to such an enterprise. The nature of mood is that by its very nature it is both sensed and shifting; images move in and out of focus and our attempts to pin down the subject compromises the life of the very thing that we are trying to understand.

For the sake of clarity, we may be best served by embracing the view that early Gnosticism relates to those traditions such as the Sethians and Valentinians which embrace varying degrees of radical dualism and the figure of the Demiurge. When we move through church history and meet figures such as the Mandeans, Mani and the Cathars, while the degree of dualism may vary both between such groups and within them), these motifs generally persist.

While it is virtually impossible not to oversimplify the relationships that these groups had with each other and their own historic forebears, as we have already touched upon, we encounter a further layer of complexity as we seek to integrate the Hermetic material rediscovered during the Renaissance. While the Hermetic corpus contains radically dualistic material, it also has material that has a more positive outlook on the material realm. As highlighted in the lives of such giants as

49

Giordano Bruno (Yates), this more integrative perspective on the physical world dovetailed well with the Renaissance's growing confidence in the scientific method.

The on-going dance between Gnostic pessimism and Hermetic optimism pervades the various magical revivals that have occurred in Europe since the Renaissance. In trying to understand contemporary manifestation of Gnosticism, we can see that this dance continues still.

In her excellent history of Independent Gnostic Churches *Gnostics, Priest and Magicians* Sibohan Houston (2009) maps out the various ecclesiastical forms that have been born as a result of attempts to evolve a more esoteric form of Christian inspired spiritual practice. Influenced by Templar lore, Freemasonry and Theosophy many of these groups have taken more traditional forms of Christian sacramental worship and used them as vehicles for re-accessing experiences of direct knowing. The adoption of these rituals is not without historical precedent, as the Valentinians made ready use of the Sacraments. For many contemporary practitioners on a Gnostic path, the structure provided by sacramental ritual and claims to apostolic succession provide a helpful means for reducing the radical subjectivity of unproven personal insight.

While the adoption of high church aesthetics may have much to do with the Catholicism of the Dutch and French contexts from which the revival churches arose, it could be argued that there are also strongly Protestant currents within the rebirth of Gnosticism. In contrast to the Roman church's emphasis on its unassailable authority to interpret scripture, the Reformation (as embodied in the figure of Martin Luther), was founded on the premise of personal revelation. As Houston (2009) brilliantly highlights, the social tumult caused by the Reformation and Counter-Reformation, led to a widespread questioning of what right a centralised ecclesiastical hegemony had to dictate conformity to Papal edicts, to which people felt little real connection.

While Luther and Calvin's emphasis on faith and the necessity of divine grace run somewhat contra to the type of knowledge-based awakening of the Gnostic path, the Protestant emphasis on the individual's ability to interpret the Bible led to the type of radical experiments of groups such as the Anabaptists and Quakers. These groups place high value on both de-centralised church structures (ultimate authority often sitting within each individual congregation) and a high value being placed on personal revelation even when it ran contra to the type of doctrinal orthodoxy embodied in the Church's creeds.

Perhaps somewhat ironically many of the contemporary Gnostic Churches who would fall under the umbrella of the Independent Sacramental movement hold together both a Catholic love of sacramental worship with a decidedly Protestant stubbornness in terms of maintaining localised diversity.

The degree to which these groups are pursuing a radical dualism is certainly open to question: Smith observed in his study of Stephan Hoeller's *Ecclesia Gnostica* that the sense of cosmic alienation associated with early Gnostic mythology has largely been located in the realm of internal psychological processes. Hoeller has responded to this and in his book *Gnosticism* (2002) has thoughtfully laid out some shared principles that he feels contemporary Gnostic practitioners can be viewed as sharing. Hoeller makes clear that such principles should be viewed as "'Flashes of Vision Glorious' rather than as a statement of religious tenets in the conventional mode" (pg. 187). These include:

"1. There is an original and transcendental spiritual unity from which emanated a vast manifestation of pluralities.
The manifest universe of matter and mind was created not by the original spiritual unity but by spiritual beings possessing inferior powers..."

The list goes on for some thirteen points and while I have huge admiration for Hoeller's work, I'm not sure to what degree my personal world-view and gnostic explorations align with these principles.

Given the rich array of groups that the early Church Fathers got upset about, it is quite likely that these early explorers had a wide diversity of insights, beliefs and practices connected to their communities. While it is only right that we try and apply a fair degree of precision to what Gnostic experience entails, a range of approaches that accounts for differing human temperaments and local contexts seems quite in keeping with what was happening during early church history.

The Gnostic Magician

While some contemporary followers of a gnostic path find consolation in the types of sacramental mysticism born out of the French Gnostic revival and the Liberal Catholic tradition, in seeking a "lived experience" of gnosis, I chose the more anarchic path of ritual experimentation known as Chaos Magic. This form of freestyle ritual magic sought to reinvigorate the dusty pseudo-masonry of many magical orders by injecting them with a heady fusion of punk rock energy and quantum mechanical insights. Much has been written about the nature of Chaos Magic, and for those wanting to understand it more fully I would recommend the works of Pete Carroll, as well as Phil Hine, and *The Book of Baphomet* by Nikki Wyrd and Julian Vayne. Of course I would also highly commend my own book *Chaos Craft* that I co-wrote with the brilliant Mr. Vayne.

While I wouldn't assume that all Chaos Magicians are Gnostics in the sense we have been considering thus far, I think that they do seek to work with the issues that we have highlighted. In contrast to most "believers", magicians are often those who actively seek to explore dualities and are willing to get their hands dirty in the process of exploring a potential synthesis.

The tensions that the magician might explore can be manifold: light and darkness, love and hate, the known and the unknown, the transcendent and immanent. The dynamic excitement experienced in the interplay between these apparent dualities is what fuels the art and science of magic. What we experience in being embodied and feeling the pull of the mysterious or transcendent can fuel our curiosity and the alchemy of self-transformation. The interplay of longed for ideal and pragmatic action create a hermetic frisson via which new realities might be born.

Now while this all appears very lofty and dynamic, it's reasonable to ask what this looks like in practice. What does the actual process of ritual creativity involve? For me personally I am engaged in an on-going journey of exploration, research and poetic inspiration as I seek to make deeper sense of the material that I'm digging into.

Anyhow, I thought I'd provide a recent example of such ritual praxis that probably gives you a feel for how we go about such work. Such ritual outlines are not meant to be prescriptive; rather they are serving suggestions to inspire your own innovation and creativity.

The purpose of this ritual was to creative an environment in which the concept of divine wisdom could be explored utilising the Gnostic figure of Sophia. Via the use of both poetry and meditative technologies, we were seeking new insight regarding holy wisdom and encouraging a sense of deep listening as to how future work should proceed:

A Mindful Mass to Sophia

Opening with a singing bowl (or a bell) rung clockwise, once to each of the 8 directions.

"We begin in Silence and Space
The realm of the Pleroma
The marriage of Darkness and Light."
8 breaths taken by all particpants together.
"In the pregnant space of reflection
Wisdom is born
Glowing deep blue against the blackness
Silver Star points glow
As the holy Aeon descends
And gives birth to life.
Selah

20 minutes Mindfulness practice – using the physical sensation of breathing as an anchor for awareness and gently surrendering thoughts, feelings and bodily sensations as they arise. Once we have acknowledged them, we return our attention to the breath.

"Wisdom makes manifest
An outflowing of the multiple and the complex
The Craftsman makes the World
Soul glows and breaths:
"I was sent forth from the power,
and I have come to those who reflect upon me,
and I have been found among those who seek after me.

Icon of St. Sophia

Look upon me, you who reflect upon me,
and you hearers, hear me.
You who are waiting for me, take me to yourselves.
And do not banish me from your sight.
And do not make your voice hate me, nor your hearing.
Do not be ignorant of me anywhere or any time. Be on your
guard!
Do not be ignorant of me.
For I am the first and the last.
I am the honored one and the scorned one.
I am the whore and the holy one.
I am the wife and the virgin.
I am the mother and the daughter.
I am the members of my mother.
I am the barren one
and many are her sons.
I am she whose wedding is great,
and I have not taken a husband.
I am the midwife and she who does not bear.
I am the solace of my labour pains.
I am the bride and the bridegroom,
and it is my husband who begot me.
I am the mother of my father
and the sister of my husband
and he is my offspring...
I am the silence that is incomprehensible
and the idea whose remembrance is frequent.
I am the voice whose sound is manifold
and the word whose appearance is multiple.
I am the utterance of my name."

(Excerpt from Thunder Perfect Mind.)

Trance drumming.

[During this ritual we had three drummers all using the technique outlined by Michael Harner, where trance is induced through the use of a consistent drum beat of around 200 beats per minute. This drumming generally lasted between 10-15 minutes.]

After the trance period and drumming ceases, the following words are spoken:

"The many forms beget Joy
But also the forgetting of our original face,
We give thanks for these moments of stillness and
remembering!
Wisdom calls:
"Does not wisdom call out?
Does not understanding raise her voice?
[2] At the highest point along the way,
where the paths meet, she takes her stand;
[3] beside the gate leading into the city,
at the entrance, she cries aloud:
[4] "To you, O people, I call out;
I raise my voice to all humanity.
[5] You who are simple, gain prudence;
you who are foolish, set your hearts on it.
[6] Listen, for I have trustworthy things to say;
I open my lips to speak what is right.
[7] My mouth speaks what is true,
for my lips detest wickedness.
[8] All the words of my mouth are just;
none of them is crooked or perverse.
[9] To the discerning all of them are right;
they are upright to those who have found knowledge.

[10] Choose my instruction instead of silver,
knowledge rather than choice gold,"

Proverbs 8:1-10

Close with three bells.

In Praise of Part-Made Gods

In my own work as a magician, I find myself attracted to those depictions of the Demiurge that reflect something of the alchemical tension innate to a more awakened encounter with the human dilemma.

I think it's fair to observe that I spend a lot of time thinking about God. This has been going on for some time (probably the last 35 years) and I don't imagine it's going to stop anytime soon.

A friend of mine who I play lots of music with asked me whether I "believed" in God, and while I've made some valiant attempts at doing so in the past, I felt unable to answer conclusively. Famously when asked this question, Carl Jung answered that he didn't believe that there was a God rather he "knew" there was. Familiarity with his biography enables us to know that Jung was a fairly seasoned Gnostic explorer at the point he made that comment, and based on his reception of *The Seven Sermons to the Dead*, it is unlikely that his deity of choice was of an orthodox variety.

In contrast to either creedal formulations or some distant "unmoved mover", for Jung the God that seemed to encapsulate the endeavour of the Gnostic explorer, was that strange bird Abraxas. Abraxas, like Baphomet, is one of those Gods whose queer visage keeps popping up in esoteric lore, while at the same time being very difficult to categorise. Research will provide some insights into the roles that he played/plays within a whole

61

host of occult traditions - this strange cockerel (and sometimes lion) headed being with its serpentine "legs" is viewed as an Aeon by some, and as an Archon or even the Demiurge by others. His number (using Greek Gematria) being 365, along with his association with the seven classical planets, connect him to both the round of the year and the physical cosmos.

For Jung, Abraxas represented a movement beyond dualism. No longer is the divine image split into a good Lord and an evil Devil; rather the mysteries of godhead are held within the complex iconography of Abraxas:

> *"Abraxas speaketh that hallowed and accursed word which is life and death at the same time. Abraxas begetteth truth and lying, good and evil, light and darkness in the same word and in the same act. Therefore is Abraxas terrible."*

The Seven Sermons to the Dead (Hoeller 1982)

Abraxas

When one meditates on the most commonly found cockerel headed form of Abraxas, we cannot but be struck by the bizarre chimera-like quality of the image. The body of a man is topped by the head of a solar cockerel (possibly symbolizing foresight and vigilance), while from under "his" concealing skirts, strange chthonic serpents come wriggling forth. This cosmic hybrid seems to be holding together the transcendent and immanent, solar and night side. Viewed through my late-Modern lens I am both awed and unsettled by the sense of internal tension that this God seems to embody.

My own attraction to strange gods is hardly new territory - that monstrous hybrid Baphomet has long been jabbing at my consciousness as I've sought to make sense of life's dissolving and coming back together. For me both Abraxas and Baphomet represent something of the core paradox that many of us experience in trying to make sense of the world.

Most attempts at constructing "big theories" (metanarratives if you like) are designed to make sense of the universe that we live within. The success or failure of any such world views seems to be largely determined either by their followers' ability to manage nuance and complexity, or conversely their naivety and willingness to block out new information. However, for those of us who are seeking to promote some form of cognitive liberty, it seems inevitable that at some point we are going to have to develop deeper strategies for managing complexity, paradox and the types of uncertainty that such realities often give birth to.

We have previously considered the way in which the duality and tension that exists within many Gnostic myths potentially trigger the awakening of consciousness; and in many ways these iconic images of Abraxas and Baphomet are little different. The juxtaposition of apparent opposites and the sense of movement that they contain speak to us of dynamism and process rather than fixed Platonic certainties. Whether via weird cosmologies or shape-shifting iconography, these gnostic riddles push us to the edges of comprehension and certainty. In seeking to engage with such material we often experience a profound unease and yet for the intrepid explorer such discomfort can trigger the types of "strange loops" that arguably enable the evolution of consciousness.

This circular, iterative use of myth and paradox leads us away from certainties that cannot bear the weight of new insight, rather we are asked to engage in an unfolding process of becoming of both ourselves and our perception of the numinous.

One such example of openness and evolutionary fluidity is the brilliant aeonic litany contained within the *Mass of Chaos B*, which provides us with a vivid example of how such evolution continues to occur:

"*In the first aeon, I was the Great Spirit.*
In the second aeon, Men knew me as the Horned God, Pangenitor Panphage.
In the third aeon, I was the Dark One, the Devil.
In the fourth aeon, Men know me not, for I am the Hidden One.

In this new aeon, I appear before you as Baphomet.
The God before all gods who shall endure to the end of the Earth!"

(Carroll 1987)

The images of both Abraxas and Baphomet that are most familiar to us, provide vivid pictorial depictions of the cosmic balancing act that we are engaged in. Humanoid bodies mutate with animal heads and transgendered bodies, as arms point at balance, or bear the whips and keys of our deliverance. For me these glyphs are road maps for becoming; the path of the demiurge being a journey through the reality of our lives, not simply away from it. As much as the realm of matter and the body may provide challenges and obstacles, this is the place we find ourselves, and where the work needs to happen.

Working with Part-Made Gods

Magicians are often those who choose to walk the treacherous path of transmuting those substances which others seek to avoid. The initiate's vows of "Daring, Willing, Knowing and Keeping Silent" challenge them to confront those obstacles within themselves formed by either genetic make-up or environmental conditioning. Arguably part of the 'Great Work' that we pursue in daring to "immanentize the eschaton' is the transformation of those aspects of ourselves that we could view as negative or Archonic, in order to make them Aeonic opportunities of further becoming and evolution.

For me, as a gnostic explorer and magician, I am drawn to these fluid gods of transformation precisely because they mirror the project of personal integration that I find myself wrestling with. On some level such an admission may seem like high narcissism, but I believe that a degree of honest self-reflection is warranted as we walk this path. Often we choose (and create) the gods most like ourselves as we seek to both make sense of our current experiences and also in our aspiration to become something more, something greater that we currently are. As a magician who is continually seeking to explore and understand the role that belief has in shifting consciousness, I also have a strong suspicion that this is far from one-way traffic i.e. our gods are feeding on us as much as we are feeding on them!

The need and desire to feed is for many of us, an uncomfortable aspect of our existence on earth that we might want to hide from. At a basic biological level, in order to survive, humans need to consume, destroy and absorb the life of something else. As much as we may want to whitewash the process, our day-to-day survival is premised on a degree of violence. Once we step outside the boundaries of 'civilisation', we quickly comprehend that we also can become the hunted as well as the hunter; such are the dynamics of the biosphere. Awareness of this principle may well influence our dietary and lifestyle choices, but it remains nonetheless.

For those seeking to explore more magical perspectives on the world, such awareness may also extend to how feeding occurs on an energetic level. In the work of Gurdjieff and other Fourth Way teachers we find the idea of reciprocal feeding; i.e. everything in the universe feeds on, and in turn is fed upon, energetically. To me this feels decidedly vampiric and as long as the feeding is mutual, it may be a helpful metaphor for understanding our relationship with the any imagined numinous realm.

Any scan of the Internet will provide a startling array of individuals and groups seeking to engage with Vampire and Otherkin identities as a means for making sense of their lives (I have written at greater length about these themes in the book "Gods and Monsters" edited by Michael Kelly). However clumsy we may view these attempts to engage with these potent archetypal images, at its best the Vampire represents a conscious engagement with the dynamic of feeding, in order to maximize its potential for wellbeing and the pursuit of initiatory goals.

It feels less than coincidental that the popularity of the Vampire myth in Western society paralleled an increased awareness of many Asian religious traditions that make more explicit reference to the subtle body, and the possibility of energetic exchange. Time does not currently permit a detailed examination of these sources, but those alchemical practices broadly described as tantric or Taoist often dealt with the cultivation and movement of subtle energy and the physical uses of bodily elixirs. Any contemporary explorer of the vampiric would be wise to integrate the insights of such traditions when evolving their own magical experiments.

Feeding need not be parasitic and there are many models of magical practice that promote an approach that is far more symbiotic and consensual (insights may well be gained from the devotional work undertaken by many practitioners working with African traditional religions). The idea of feeding is hardly new within the realm of religious expression. Whether it be a Catholic high mass, a Vaishnava's offering of Prashadam (sacred food) to Krishna and Radha or a Heathen sumbel, the use of ingested food to express faith is as old as humanity itself. How we eat and what we eat, are unavoidable expressions of who we are and what we want to become - this is true of both our shopping habits and also the way we use food in the context of our own spiritual journeys. What more powerful way to connect to your god, than ingesting their "body and blood" and fusing them with your own physiology?

We need to pick our gods and heroes with care in that our devotions are acts of feeding that generate seismic ripples within our psyches. Others (e.g. social media and advertising) may well have a strong interest in what we are 'fed' and what 'feeds upon' us. For those of us seeking to cultivate a certain degree of cognitive liberty, we may well need to employ our best banishing practices in order to create the type of space that promotes our freedom.

Beelzebub and the New Hermetics

While I personally feel that the wider Gnostic community benefits hugely from having a variety of ritual expressions in our attempt to work with these ideas in a contemporary context, e.g. Sacramental type churches, free-form magical practice groups, masonic lodges and meditation groups, it seems that very few are not to some extent informed by the insights of G.I. Gurdjieff and the Fourth Way teachings.

Gurdjieff

Even a cursory glance at either Gurdjieff's own writing or that of Ouspensky (cf. "In Search of the Miraculous"), will demonstrate the complexity of the teachings both in terms of their cosmology and ontology. With its deliberate obscuration, coined phrases and frankly bonkers pseudo-gnostic mythos, the Work provides us with a set of ideas that are as intriguing and infuriating as the twilight language of tantra.

In short, the Fourth Way Work views humanity's normal state of being as machine-like. The demands of culture, family, our bodies and our lives have made us automaton. The demands are the archons of our time in causing us to forget who we truly are. We are on autopilot, we are asleep. The aim of the Work is wake us from this sleep. The existence of our soul cannot be presumed upon, it must be worked for, and fought-for Soul must be created. But how is one to accomplish such a task?

Gurdjieff recognised that throughout humanity's history we have sought to connect to God/Holy Guardian Angel/True Self etc. He believed that these efforts could be categorised via the centre or starting point from which they began their journey. In short, these paths are the way of the body (the fakir), the way of the heart (the monk) and the way of the mind (the yogi). Whatever benefit may have been gained in the past through the pursuit of these means, in our age and within a life lived outside of monastery walls we need something more. For Gurdjieff this is the Fourth Way.

The Fourth Way is the way of the sly man: the one who seeks to harmonize body, heart and mind as they seek to awaken solar consciousness. The Work challenges us to Self-remember, to become more awake within the bodymind. The methods we may employ, like Beelzebub, are legion, but the goal of seeking soulful awakened depth remains.

Postmodern magical types like me are always harking on about "the map not being the territory", but we still need maps. Frankly, if I were lost I'd rather make use of a sketchy map than none at all. Now maps can always be improved upon and there is the danger that we spend so much time looking at the bloody map that we miss the incoming weather front.... Maps hopefully provide us with a sense of where we are in the landscape, and where we need to travel in order to reach our destination.

Magic without a teleological goal can easily descend into what Chogyam Trungpa called "spiritual materialism". Without some general sense of direction, we can end up endlessly turning in circles, covering the same territory and end up feeling completely exhausted (sound familiar?). The Work potentially provides us with a helpful (if at times eccentric) map, for avoiding just such a pitfall.

I find the division of the Work into the three centres, and the three ways of being, as a helpful way of gaining a holistic perspective on our Gnostic endeavours. What follows is some reflection on what Gnostic work on the three centres has meant for me.

The Gnostic Mind...

In the history of Gnostic revivalism over the past 150 years, much emphasis has been placed on ecclesiastical structure and the role of sacramentalism within the churches birthed from this impulse. In my view, the form that these groups adopted partially relates to the French Catholic context from which this revival emerged, but it is also connected to a belief that the sacraments of the church provide a powerful and established means through which gnosis can flow (see the work of Leadbeater and the Liberal Catholic tradition).

While I might personally struggle with some of the aesthetic and structural aspects of such an approach, far be it from me to criticise the rich tradition such churches embody, and the benefits that others might gain from it.

While we must remain awake to not allowing fine robes and titles to distract us from the true work of gaining gnosis, as a Chaos magician I more aware than most that all of our spiritual traditions are 'made up' at some point in response to our encounter with Mystery! While I may not connect to forms of practice that are rooted in the language and ritual of the historic church, if you find that helpful by all means pursue it.

My own approach to Gnosis has been decidedly less wordy and formal than either the ceremonies of Sacramentalism or the pseudo-masonic rubric of the Golden Dawn tradition. In contrast I have sought to utilise a form of 'deep listening' practice, that has its origins in both contemplative prayer and Buddhist inspired mindfulness practices.

It's probably fair to observe that my own approach and ecclesiology resemble that of the early Quaker and Shaker traditions (though sadly with less excellent furniture construction involved). On a personal note, I have always found it somewhat comical that while I no longer call myself a Christian, I still seem rather wedded to the Anabaptist tradition, with its emphasis on simple aesthetics and the central importance of the local congregation.

Working with Stillness

In my view, both the gnostic cosmologies and the insights of the Buddha's Four Noble Truths were born out of a profound unease regarding the pain of human experience. Mindfulness practice is far from attaining imagined utopias, or having to adopt beliefs that jar with our experience of reality. In contrast it lays down the rather stark challenge of staying with the present moment and whatever arises for us in that moment. In my own experience, in being attentive to what arises, and the dynamic of that process, accessing greater insight or gnosis becomes possible.

What stillness-based approaches allow us to do par excellence is to create a sense of distance between ourselves as thinkers and the thoughts we have. For the mindfulness practitioner such a challenge is less about the suppression of unwanted thought, rather it seeks a more neutral 'just noticing' that acknowledges that as thought arises, so eventually it will dissipate. This stuff gets kicked-up because it is in the nature of the human mind to do so; we can get caught-up in trying to construct a coherent narrative from it, or we can wait to see if a deeper, less reactive wisdom emerges.

In recent studies focused on positive psychology much has been made of the role of flow or fluidity as an optimal state in which a person is able to access a greater sense of personal happiness and creativity. Somewhat paradoxically, mindfulness practice appears to enable this through a greater acceptance of life's unpredictability, and the sense of uncertainty that this can cause for us. With its historic roots in a Buddhist philosophy that saw the challenging nature of life as being unavoidable, mindfulness practice seeks to provide us with skills for managing our internal struggles more effectively. With its insights into how to work with both impermanence and our sense of existential dissatisfaction (Dukkha), the Buddhist tradition has much to offer those of us seeking to evolve a contemporary gnostic pathway.

While both the Buddhist and gnostic perspectives sought to grapple with how we humans respond to our experience of suffering, the Buddha's teachings do highlight the danger of trying too hard to locate cosmic causation. As illustrated by the parable of the soldier injured by an arrow, we should focus less on who shot the arrow and more on our need to deal with the reality of being wounded. Those of us trying to engage with gnostic creation myths should probably heed such sage advice. The teaching stories of the Gnostics may help elucidate our human experience, but sometimes the truly wise realisation is that there might be limits on what we can truly know, and, that we have to learn to live with uncertainty.

Gnostic Pathworking

As well as utilising more passive, receptive states of consciousness, it can also be helpful to have some more active, change focused strategies in one's personal magical armory. In seeking greater access to the type of spacious stillness that we might associate with the Pleroma, the Sethian Gnostics sought to employ a type of active pathworking or visualization technique that enabled them to explore the internal terrain of the psyche, in the belief that it paralleled the aspirant's journey up and through the various Aeonic strata:

> *"The human mind is a kind of miniature representation of the aeons that emanate from the ultimate God... For this reason, the Gnostic could also contemplate God by contemplating his or her own intellect..."*

Brakke, The Gnostics, p80

This seems to reflect something of the Hermetic insight, "as above so below". What I also find interesting (and encouraging!) is that such an approach makes few grandiose claims of access to immediate mind blowing epiphanies; rather it recommends repeated and reflective exploration of this territory as a preparation for full union with the divine.

In working with such cosmic schema we allow the construction of an internal psychogeography. These maps can become constrictive over time, but at their best they provide a means for making greater sense of incoming gnosis, and are tools for integrating new insights more effectively. For those of you who make use of maps such as the Qabalistic Tree of Life, or the Norse World Tree, the value of using this type of internal landscape will be familiar.

These big, beautiful brains of ours can be realms of both joyous discovery and confusing torment. In considering the project of integration we must remain alive to the challenge of seeking to bring together work with both the body and the emotions so as to ensure a sustainability to the insights we gain.

The Gnostic Body...

For the Gnostics, our relationship with our body has not always been an easy one. The problems of pain and impermanence, that played such a central role in the development of Gnostic dualism, most likely originated in their experience of the body within the natural world. We have already spent time thinking about how theodicy, or the problem of evil, contributed to the evolution of Gnostic cosmologies. If disease and death demonstrated the imperfection of the demiurge's realm, then it would seem likely that the strategies of either asceticism or antinomian excess were evidence of a potentially hostile attitude towards the body.

While we may concede that many Gnostics viewed the divine pneumatic spark as being trapped within the material realm, as contemporary magical practitioners exploring what we might learn from them, I believe that it is wise to pay attention to what they did as much as what they may have believed. Often the 'lived experience' of what people actually did can help us gain insights into the complex relationship that they had with apparently straightforward ideas.

Dance like the Pleroma's watching!

In the Gnostic scripture *The Acts of John* we have a really interesting description of ritual dance and liturgy that is alleged to have taken place during the Last Supper:

> *So he commanded us to make a circle, holding one another's hands, and he himself stood in the middle....*
> *I will pipe, dance all of you! Amen....*
> *An eightfold power is singing with us. Amen*
> *The whole universe takes part in the dancing. Amen*
> *He who does not dance, does not know what is being done. Amen.*
> **The Acts of John Section 94-95.**

Some scholars believe that this is most likely a ritual text that was part of the style of worship employed by the Johannite community. In seeking to fathom the myth of incarnation, it is hardly surprising that we are met with the possibility of Jesus and the apostles using their bodies to move, both in celebration, and to dissipate the mounting tension of what was to come.

It may seem like a somewhat obvious point to make, but generally as human beings the realisations and ecstasies of the mind and heart bubble over into these bodies we inhabit. Personally I would question the true depth of any revelation that did not impact upon all dimensions of our being.

Even if we chose to limit our attention to phenomena within the Christian tradition, we can consider traditions such as those of the Shakers and the Pentecostals, and the role that movement and dance had as people sought to express a form of gnostic experience that moves through and beyond intellectual insight alone.

As someone exploring the Gnostic material through the less orthodox route of a Chaos Magically inspired form of Witchcraft, I find that dance and improvised movement have been highly beneficial in helping me make sense of what might be going on.

In seeking to loosen the tensions and defenses that often get located in what Wilhelm Reich described as "body armour", I often have a sense of a deeper instinctive knowing emerging in and through the body.

When I move in response to the music my self-consciousness slowly melts away. This type of 'shape-shifting' may well relate to the way in which the body allows us to process aspects of the self that the conscious mind struggles to make sense of. Interesting research is beginning to explore this territory, and it may be that the 'darker', more instinctive drivers of the early or reptilian brain get processed more effectively when we actively engage the body. As I dance I often feel that in my messy embodiment, I am making sense of my early and deepest drives (for more on this see *The Compassionate Mind* by Paul Gilbert and Peter Levine's work on trauma).

For those interested in exploring this territory further I would recommend Bradford Keeney's book *Shaking Medicine,* and Jan Fries' book *Seidways.*

Ritual Space

The very act of ritual speaks to and through our bodies via symbol and movement, set within space and time. By making use of colour, light and sound we engage the senses, and vibrate words through our flesh. Even the most apparently dualistic Gnostics made use of baptisms and the Eucharist as a way to bring God into the body. Rarely do we rely on cognition alone, rather we anchor experience through the sensual. Perhaps in seeking to work with any sense of distance and dualism, part of the answer lies in bringing a greater degree of awareness to what we experience in the body.

The type of alchemical process that I'm seeking to describe at a microcosmic level is similar in many ways to the dynamic and subtle interplay that occurs between the Pleroma, Sophia and the Demiurge within Gnostic mythology. However much the Gnostic myths might highlight the dilemmas experienced by inhabiting human form, we must also remain awake to the reality of a sensual ritual praxis that provides a more creative and lateral approach to exploring the mysteries.

Often the rich theatre of a ritual and the items on an altar reveal as much about a tradition's theology as does a scriptural text.

These experiences of worship and practice may be inspired by understanding and cognition, but they are felt in our bodies and stir the depths of our emotions.

Gateway Tentacles

The Gnostic Heart...

In reflecting on how we as Gnostic explorers might develop contemporary practice, I have been grappling with the dilemma of how we might reconcile the radical dualism of some gnostic groups (e.g. the Sethians), with an experience of the material world that acknowledges its rich complexity and the sensual pleasures associated with it.

In my own explorations I have found something of a mediating position via the 'soft' dualism contained in the *Corpus Hermeticum*, which sought to incorporate a more emanation-based model. In keeping with the insights of much Neoplatonic thinking, the light of the Godhead still permeates the lower realms of matter, even if in a more dilute fashion. The crafted realm of the demiurge contains a messy diversity that our ordered minds sometimes struggle with. For our Universe to exist at all, it seems that it must operate with a beautiful savagery that we may find bewildering.

As a chaos magician I am thankfully spared the dilemma of whether such speculations are ultimately true (apparently "nothing/everything is true"), but my desire to explore this territory continues to be far more than mere hipster paradigm shifting. Perhaps as evidence of my human curiosity, these mythic riddles act like Zen koans in breaking apart my all-too linear attempts to comprehend. Perhaps the genius of much Gnostic mythology is that in contemplating its paradoxical nature, so it triggers new, more lateral insights. The bearing of such tensions is far from the path of the armchair magician; in seeking wisdom this alchemical process forces us to confront the limits of what we know. Like Socrates we proclaim:

"The only true wisdom is in knowing that you know nothing."

If the path of the Gnostic is primarily concerned with the incoming of knowledge and startling new insight, it might lead us to conclude that it is a somewhat dry path when contrasted with the orthodoxy of a believer's faith. To some extent such a contrast is fitting, in that the Gnostics seemed to have been dissatisfied with relying on the revelations of others, instead seeking them for themselves. Such advancement seems more reliant on personal effort rather than appealing to the sentimentality of a loving God.

In my view the full implication of any gnostic insight can only be fully comprehended if we are able to integrate it at both a physical and emotional level. While we might contrast the Gnostic path with the more faith and emotion focused emphasis of the believer, we must remain awake to the central importance of the heart in seeking to cultivate wisdom.

When we seek to comprehend the tension that is central to so much of the Gnostic schema, it is the figure of Sophia or Divine Wisdom that provides some reconciliation between apparent duality. She acts as the mediator between the lofty aspiration of the Pleroma and the embodiment of the demiurge. In the ritual poem that we use at our monthly Zen Hearth meetings, we declare:

"We come seeking Gnosis
And the Wisdom to apply it"

The path of Sophia seeks to integrate any insights gained via gnosis and make them manifest through right attitude and action. As with Hegel's conception of thesis, antithesis and the reconciling synthesis, so the Pleroma and Demiurge represent a polarity that Sophia balances and contains.

In my own efforts to work with the heart from a Gnostic perspective I have sought to engage both artistic creativity and less goal focused magical practices. The setting up of an altar space to Sophia allows me a form of shy invocation – an engagement with the senses, a gentle simmering of devotion that seeks to avoid some brash cut-and-paste results magic. In these reflections I'm drawn to past memories of Ruach, Shekinah and the image of Wisdom calling out on the street corners:

"Hear how Wisdom calls
and understanding lifts her voice.
She takes her stand at the crossroads,
By the wayside at the top of the hill...
She cries aloud:
"It is to you I call,
To all humanity I appeal"

Proverbs 8:1-4

Whatever text one chooses, be it ancient or new, the act of Lectio Divina (conscious meditation and incubation of a verse) allows the Gnostic explorer the possibility for new insights and wisdom to grow. We need to create space for this process to mature and to take the brave step in admitting that we don't know or understand something, or even that our previous knowledge needs to be unlearnt.

Seeking the Muse

To seek gnosis via creative means often allows the intrepid explorer access to the unconscious and a manifestation of wisdom that can potentially hold apparent polarities in dynamic tension. Whether via visual art, music, dance or other means, to create is to channel the incoming genius through the body and to infuse it with impulses that express soul. Whichever medium we choose, these creative acts become vehicles of incarnation as we take the heady and ethereal and combine it with the blood and dirt of our endeavors. Our creations become *Gnostic Machines* through which we can communicate mystery to our world, as I have written elsewhere:

> "*Dark Matter Flows,*
> *Flows through Gnostic Machinery.*
> *Metaphysical truths,*
> *Now patent absurdities.*
> *Strip it back,*
> *Strip it right back,*
> *And journey into Space,*
> *Remembering your true Self,*
> *Seeing your original face*"

To create means taking risk and moving from the imagined ideal (the Pleroma) to the messy, dynamic reality of what we can deliver (the Demiurge). Rarely are our first results our best, but in seeking to master any craft we can learn much about ourselves.

To bare the tension of such polarities is a path to Wisdom, and emulates Sophia herself:

> "It is I who am restraint and unrestraint.
> It is I who am joining: and dissolution:
> It is I who am persistence:
> And it is I who am weakening.
> It is I who am descent:
> And it is to me that people ascend."

The Thunder, Perfect Mind

Interlude - Your Path to Gnosis...

In reading Hoeller's list of possible commonalities for those of us seeking the Gnostic path, I was struck by the interesting terrain that lies between beliefs and inspiration. While Hoeller is clear that these are potentially shared concepts rather than faith tenets, I will have to own my own baggage in relation to anything that looks like a creedal statement. While such defining traits are undoubtedly helpful in trying to capture accurately the shared perspectives of the earliest Gnostics, rather than viewing them as a mandate for reconstructionism, I choose to view them as triggers for inspiration.

"You have your way. I have my way. As for the right way, the correct way, and the only way, it does not exist."

Nietzsche

A good friend of my once observed that we should pay more attention to what we find ourselves doing rather than what we think we should be doing. What my friend (who is both a therapist and magician) was pointing towards was that we often cause ourselves suffering through the endless cycle of searching, aspiration and acquisition. "If I just gain mastery of x, acquire this book or undertake this training then I will know who I am and what I'm supposed to be doing here!" Sadly this doesn't really work does it? We might gain a temporary sugar-high from rebranding ourselves or spending far too much on fine books (or wines), but if your anything like me we end up caught in a solipsistic loop where we end up exhausted (and frankly bored) by our endless self-narrative.

My friend's theory was that if we pause for a moment and reflect on the things that we actually do and enjoy doing (hence why we keep doing them), then we are probably getting close to understanding something about what we really desire. Desire often gets a bad press, but personally I feel that our problems with distraction and consumerism are often our attempts to flee from the cost that our real heart-longings might ask of us. The quick-fix is really no fix at all and contrasts radically with the type of awakening and attentive self-listening that will allow us to look down to the soil in which our personal roots are really bedded.

Such self-reflection is rarely easy and in making the effort to 'tune-in' to these realities, we may have to turn-down or reject the versions of ourselves that others may want us to buy into. This willed antinomianism allows the creation of a space in which we might experience a greater sense of cognitive liberty in experimenting with our dreams. This is the demarcation of the magical circle – a lab in which we create the optimal conditions for self-examination. In waking up to "what we find ourselves doing" I have often opted for a period of elective self-limitation. In a world where endless choice and speed are valued, a period of monastic retreat often allows the cultivation of clarity.

As we push our hands down into the dark soil of our unconscious, we risk the possibility of contacting some of the core aspects of what drives us and what things cause us to feel most alive. The discovery of this dark matter is rarely linear and the value of art, dreams and synchronicities should not be underestimated. Often the untidy syncretism of our altar spaces reveal more to us than our ordered book shelves.

In reconnecting to the 'what is' of the moment, rather than becoming stuck we create the possibility of emergence coming from a place of depth. Stirred by the memory of some conversations with a Setian Priest, I keep returning to the concept of how important need-fire is in the pursuit of my own initiatory work. Whether one self-defines as a magician or not, one of the primary indicators of whether a goal will reach fruition relates to the degree we are motivated by burning need. To follow a path of the basis of whim or fashion may provide a temporary distraction, but it is unlikely to adequately fuel significant transformation.

In many ways these observations connect to the magical work that Julian and I outlined in *Chaos Craft*. In contrast to the often hyper-accelerated go-getting that one might associate with Chaos Magic, this project has sought to integrate the inescapability of the moment made manifest in time and the spirit of place. We make no claims to lineage or secrets shared on Grandma's knee, rather this is a Witchcraft born of a connection to a raw coastline, the beating of drums and a desire to awaken.

This is the Witchcraft we found ourselves doing; a search for gnosis generated by a search for greater freedom.

To look into the mirror and truly see ourselves requires real bravery. To let go of the script of how it should be and to ask "What is it that I find myself doing...?" is truly revelatory. It may reveal the nature and extent of our current desires and also our need to escape from the current constraints that block our unfolding. There are no simple answers but, it is a beginning.

Our Future Magical Selves

Occasionally I have the privilege of being part of a lecture series for people (both lay and professional) exploring themes in therapy. In preparing one such lecture on the interface between therapy and spirituality, I had cause to revisit some of psychotherapies' heavy hitters and the maps that they devised in seeking to understand approaches that might broadly be called "Transpersonal".

On a superficial reading Freud was a good rationalist/scientist in presenting his psychoanalytic insights to the world. He viewed religion as repressive and as a result of psychological immaturity: God being an illusion that is improvable and that faith in him/her is a defence against "the crushing superiority of nature." On closer analysis, when we reflect on the degree to which he relied on the mysterious realm of the unconscious, we still have to consider that he faces similar problems around provability that a religious person does. While the analytic tools of free association and dream analysis may be very helpful, they are still based on a faith position.

Anyone interested in exploring transpersonal perspectives on psychology is going to have to deal with the therapeutic giant that is Carl Gustav Jung. The acolyte of Freud who broke with him over his belief that humanity's goal was for meaning rather than pleasure alone, Jung's own crisis of faith was to become axiomatic in his quest to understand the process of human individuation.

Running contra to the current obsession with evidence-based approaches to therapy, the concepts that Jung developed were largely as a result of his own Gnostic/spiritual encounters. In concert with his own therapeutic practice, these experiences contributed to the evolution of a decidedly rich vein of ideas; the Collective Unconscious, Archetypes, Synchronicity... the list goes on. In my view the descriptive language of Western occultism would be noticeably poorer without the presence of the Swiss hexenmeister!

Moving on to the insights of the humanistic psychology (Maslow, Rogers, Assagioli et al) we see in their post-war optimism a rejection of the pathology driven perspectives of analytic psychotherapy, and a desire to understand more fully what constitutes "positive mental health". While Abraham Maslow's exploration of "self-actualization" sought to grapple with the outer dimensions of Self and the way in which Gnostic insights might break into consciousness, it was Assagioli that sought to map this process more fully.

In one of his letters Freud said, "I am interested only in the basement of the human being." Assagioli's desire to cultivate interest in "the whole building" of consciousness eventually lead him to formulate a therapeutic approach that he dubbed Psychosynthesis:

"That means Psychosynthesis is holistic, global and inclusive. It is not against psychoanalysis or even behavior modification but it insists that the needs for meaning, for higher values, for a spiritual life, are as real as biological or social needs. We deny that there are any isolated human problems.

Nature is always trying to re-establish harmony, and within the psyche the principle of synthesis is dominant. Irreconcilable opposites do not exist. The task of therapy is to aid the individual in transforming the personality, and integrating apparent contradictions. Both Jung and myself have stressed the need for a person to develop the higher psychic functions, the spiritual dimension."

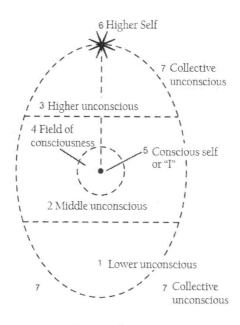

Assagioli's Egg

While I generally find over-complicated 'Maps' of the Self both difficult to use in a practical way and also quite speculative (Ken Wilber's work being a case in point!), Assagioli's egg diagram continues to be very helpful.

While time dictates that a fuller explanation of the egg must be left in the hands of Google (other search engines are available), as a Magical practitioner I am particularly interested in the insights it provides in understanding the process of personal initiation.

I think that for me as I revisited the Egg model I was able to see reflected within it some key aspects of my personal spiritual journey that remain highly resonant in terms of where I find myself today. In the lower segment of the egg, I find myself re-contacting the pagan, the ancestral and the primal. Whatever my struggles might be with regards to the overly romanticized lens of Neo-Paganism, I cannot and must not disconnect from the story of my beginnings, my context and the messy realities of embodiment. The richness of these connections and potent longings that bubble up from the unconscious are the life-blood of my magical craft. Without the dark, the earth and the drives of the Id, I potentially jeopardize both depth and mystery.

The central zone of Assagioli's map is largely concerned with the present - the work of this Moment as Toni Packer might put it. However we might conceive of the Self at the centre of our being, awareness is amoeba-like in its shifting fluidity. The preoccupations that writers I work with have with mindfulness and awakening are often interacting with this realm. What does it mean to be here? Who am I? How should I then live? These are good questions with a multiplicity of answers that are often less important than the sense of questioning and wonder that they provoke. The tools that allow us to explore this territory - mindfulness practices, body work, artistic exploration etc. are as much means for tolerating our own uncertainty as they are ways of gaining spiritual insight.

The upper realm belongs to my inner-Gnostic. For me this is the path of aspiration, guarded futurism and teleological endeavor. Magical work that has no aspiration, no real longing that it is seeking to fulfill is unlikely to sustain focus. Most of us who seek to follow an initiatory or magical path do so because we want more. We aspire to understand our past and who we are today so that we might maximize our being and pull in gnosis from our future magical selves. Nema in her excellent *Maat Magick* locates such work in the figure of N'Aton, an androgynous future Self that holds within it both our individual and collective genius. In my own explorations I have gained much from seeking to interact with this concept/being, and such workings can provide rich illustration regarding what we aspire to be and the challenges that might limit such becoming.

Assagioli's map provides us with a helpful tool for self-exploration and for me its three realms speak powerfully to the pagan, meditative and Gnostic aspects of who I am. While the map continues to not be the territory, the egg with its dashed-lines speaks of a permeability and fluidity that we as magicians can play with as we balance and counter-balance in our Great Work.

Awakening the Magical Self

Let's face it, being human can be difficult at times; not only do we have the basic needs of food, shelter and survival to contend with, but we also have to struggle with those nagging questions about "why am I here?" and "why am I still unhappy?". When faced with such dilemmas we human beings have been endlessly inventive in our attempts at brushing them under the carpet. We are endlessly trying to shift our shape in the hope that the new thing will provide the salve we seek: more food, more sex, more stuff, frankly more of anything in an attempt to anesthetise our core pain.

Many seek to manage this anxiety through the embrace of faith and the certainties that it offers. I've had my own stab at suppressing reality via the path of religious orthodoxy, but my inner heretic won out.

The path of magic is simply not suited to those who desire either a simple solution to life's mystery or are unable to withstand mind-warping bouts of existential anguish (sounds attractive doesn't it?!). To be a Mage is less a noun and more a verb, a process of ongoing exploration and refinement, in which the light of realisation moves in and out of view.

While ontological certainties may be less familiar to such intrepid explorers, it hasn't prevented us from making a multitude of maps. These may be borrowed from the religious soil from which the magician originated or they might be fresh

101

mutations based on insights gleaned from science. Whether we base our journeyings on chakras, the Tree of Life or post-Freudian models of the self, many of them seem to have a shared preoccupation with the pursuit of holism and the reconciliation of apparent opposites.

Most of the maps that I find helpful (such as Assagioli's Egg) acknowledge that our experience of human existence is profoundly coloured by a whole host of competing drives that are further complicated by our experience of linear time. Most of us are wrestling with the realities of physical survival, the questions of who we are now and our hopes and questions about life after death. To complicate matters further these drives are generally set within a timeline where we have to interpret the past (forgetting bits, idealising bits, demonising bits), experience the present (to varying degrees) and speculate on an unknown future. It's enough to give anyone a headache!

Those who practice within various forms of Chaos magic have consciously sought to engage with this maelstrom via the skilful application of apparently non-occult technologies. The present tense has an arsenal of awareness techniques brought to bear on it, while the very linearity of time is questioned as weaponised Neuro-Lingistics seek to untie knotty past traumas and whisper to our future selves so that our best futures might become possible.

While a certain degree of self-awareness thankfully prevents delusions of megalomania, what such an approach does promote is a sense of curiosity and agency. As a Magician these two traits are mutually dependent treasures; the sense of some power allows me to manage my anxiety in a way that allows a more open exploration of what the difficulty might be. So often our terror shuts us down and prevents a more open appraisal of whatever challenges are in front of us. To cultivate a more experimental, playful engagement with a situation promotes a perspective where we are allowed to be less than perfect and emphasises that our understanding is part of a learning process.

Exercise 3: Your Future Magical Self

This exercise was originally presented as a group working in our magical lodge back in 2009. This practice aims to work with our future magical selves and owes inspiration to Edred Thorsson's work on the Wode Self (found in his brilliant *Nine Doors of Midgard*) and Nema's concept of N'Aton found in her fabulous book *Ma'at Magick*.

The purpose of this practice is to allow us to consider how we wish to see ourselves change magically in the future and to provide a ritual means for integrating these changes more fully in the present.

Step 1. With a piece of paper and pen at hand, write down those qualities that you wish to see in your magical life and practice in 12 months from the current moment. What are you doing? What new skills or knowledge have you acquired? What are you wearing? What does your altar space look like? Try to be ambitious but also realistic: most effective and sustainable change comes through utilising the raw material of who you are now. We are not talking about a personality swap, but rather a process of enhancement and enrichment.

Step 2. Stand in a comfortable position and become aware of your breathing. If it aids you in visualising and doesn't cause you to fall over you can close your eyes. As your breathing naturally slows and you inhabit your body more fully, reflect on yourself as the Witch, Shaman, Gnostic, Magician, (insert relevant descriptor) which you find yourself being right now. The very fact that you walk this narrow path means that you are already brave and brilliant. Spend time reflecting on what you currently do well and give back to the world and also spend time acknowledging those aspects of yourself that might be more challenging or problematic. This version of you in this moment must not be pushed away, this dark, rich material is the soil from which the future you will be fed.

Step 3. While in this state of relaxed connectedness, begin to visualise the physical form of your future-self standing opposite you. As you imagine looking into their eyes, visualise them possessing those qualities that you will make your own. In contemplating their physical traits and the way you will engage in the world, imagine that their form begins to glow with blue light. As your visualisation becomes more vivid and focused, so the blue light becomes more intense and electrified.

Step 4. Embrace your future magical self! Activate those kinaesthetic learning processes by physically leaning into your visualised form. Absorb that blue energetic version of you and draw in those new qualities and traits. Connect to the energy of this embrace!

In the version of the ritual that I delivered within our magical group, we passed a small hand mirror around the circle and each of us spent time gazing at our own eyes in order to ground this experience more fully. In turn we passed the mirror to the person next to us and gave the blessing: "Embrace your magical self! Pass it on!"

Salvation: Within, Out, Through and Back

Models such as those proposed by Assagioli and Ken Wilber acknowledge that at differing periods in human history, the preoccupations of a given culture have significantly shaped its spiritual goals.

For example, if we view a society that has a close relationship with the cycle of the seasons in relation to agriculture, it may be unsurprising to us if aspects of their theology pay significant attention to fertility, and deities of a distinctly cthonic flavour.

This dynamic relationship between a culture and its mythology, while helpful to acknowledge, is often far from straightforward and terms of causation are rarely linear. If for example one looks at the rise of Neo-Paganism as an out-working of late Romanticism, we can view this as an attempt to counter the excessive urban mechanization of the Industrial revolution (Hutton 1999).

While contemporary Neo-Pagan theology is undoubtedly complex, I think that it would be fairly accurate to typify it as a spiritual tradition that sees salvation based predominantly **within** the realm of the natural world. While theories of the afterlife abound, a focus on magical practice and worship within the natural world promote a sense of awakening through a deepened connection to matter, rather than a move away from it (Jones and Pennick 1995).

In contrast to this emphasis on salvation within matter, most forms of Gnosticism tend to emphasize salvation as a movement out of the material world. Whatever the cause of the suffering that we currently experience within the world, the Gnostic liberation is primarily one of escape. Whether this is framed as escape from the realm of impermanent matter, or from archon induced false-consciousness, those locating their inspiration within the early Gnostic period tend to be seeking freedom from this world.

> *"Through the spiritual practice of the mysteries (sacraments) and a relentless and uncompromising striving for gnosis, humans can steadily advance toward liberation from all confinement, material and otherwise. The ultimate objective of this process of liberation is the achievement of salvific knowledge and with it, freedom from embodied existence and return to the ultimate unity."*
> *Hoeller 2002 p189*

We have already spent some time considering the Hermetic tradition as an attempt to reconcile the anti-cosmic impulse of the early Gnostics with a more positive perspective to the material realm. While the *Corpus Hermeticum* incorporates early material that represents both these perspectives, it is not until the later Hermetic material (such as *The Emerald Tablet*) where we witness a fuller synthesis of these tensions:

> *"That which is above is as that which is below.*
> *And that which is below is as that which is above.*
> *Thus are accomplished the miracles of the One."*
> *Ogilvy 2006*

The occult arts that one associates with the Hermetic tradition; lab alchemy, astrology, and Theurgic speculation, all rely to some extent on an interconnectedness between the material and spiritual realms. In contrast to the Gnostic emphasis on moving out, the transformational use of matter seems to be a movement **through** the material realm.

While the theurgic aims of Hermeticism may aim for an ultimate union with the Nous, or the Great Mind, its alchemical methodology maps out a more cyclical, iterative sense of refinement and transformation. The stages of nigredo, albedo and rubedo (black, white and red) within the Great Work speak to me of a process of ascension and eventual return.

In taking inspiration from the concepts of Transactional Analysis and the work of M. Scott Peck, we can view the way we interact with mystery as a type of developmental timeline. In such a schema, the innocence of childhood belongs to the fundamentalist, the rebellious adolescent is the ever-questioning agnostic, whereas the mystic seeks the integrating adult position. In this model, true and lasting transformation ('perfect fixity' in alchemical terms) comes not via simply rejecting the beliefs of youth in a fit of punk rock energy; rather it comes via a refined and nuanced synthesis. This experience of mystical awakening becomes not an end in itself but rather the beginning of yet another cycle of purification and change that will inevitably present its own challenges.

For me one of the most intriguing aspects of the Hermetic worldview that connects to some of the more Alien themes of the Gnostics is its emphasis on the Solar and the Galactic. In keeping with the Renaissance's newfound scientific confidence and astronomical preoccupations, the life of our planet was placed within on a vast Cosmic backdrop.

This fascination with the depths of space fits well for the Postmodern magician seeking to draw inspiration from the reservoir of Hermetic mythology. Whether it's the Magi of the gospels, the Mithraic tauroctany or the Cosmic vision of Giodarno Bruno, to place oneself within the Hermetic stream is to cast our eyes heavenwards.

New Christic Polytheism

In trying to develop a greater understanding of how Christic or gnostic imagery can be utilised in the pursuit of initiation I've recently been re-reading *Love, Sex, Fear, Death* by Timothy Wyllie. As I did so I was once again struck by the potent iconography and influence of The Process Church of the Final Judgement. The 1960s were undeniably a time of heady social ferment and cultural creativity – the love and peace idealism of the Haight Ashbury set, cross-pollinating with student unrest and a growing awareness of the inequalities that were present for many people on both sides of the Atlantic. While many were intoxicated by the popularity of spiritual traditions generically described as 'Eastern', it was perhaps surprising that through a haze of dope and incense, strode the hard-edged Gnostics of the Process.

"The Process" stood in stark contrast to the loose limbed aesthetic of the flower powered. Sporting long robes and satanically shaped beards (optional), The Process appeared to be responding to a darker, more visceral vision than many of their peers. In the nine years during which its co-founder Robert De Grimston was at the helm, the Process integrated some initial insights gained from Scientology with a radical re-working of Judeo-Christian mythology.

Responding to a series of visionary experiences gained while in Mexico, the group set out a polarity in which Christ, Satan, Jehovah and Lucifer were in dynamic tension with each other. As is so often the case, this cosmology then provided much of the focus for initiatory work within the Process. Processeans would often identify which of the specific primary deities reflected their core psychological profile, and in doing so which balancing quality they might need to pursue in seeking integration.

I would highly recommend Wyllie's book, not only for its brilliant collection of original Process art work and magazine articles, but also its reflections on how group dynamics function within new religious movements. While it undoubtedly displayed many traits that raise concerns about cult-like behaviour, for those of us interested in how Luciferian/Gnostic imagery has been utilised in initiatory work, they provide us with much to learn from.

In our engagement with the Gnostic narrative we have already given some thought to the potential value of trying to view the players on that mythic stage from a more systemic perspective. While the Gnostic scriptures provide us with a theological model that is full of dualism and oppositional tensions, it can also be helpful to view them with a more pantheon-focused or polytheistic lens. Whatever beliefs we might hold regarding the ultimate unity (or not) of the Mystery, the reality is that as humans we tend to adopt religious frameworks that allow for some allowance of multiplicity and complexity.

Historians of religious history might consider the virtual impossibility of maintaining absolute monotheism. However desirable the Oneness of God may be at a philosophical level, the messy phenomena of how we do our religions seems to point toward a more team based approach. Whether it's the 99 names of Allah or the evolution of the doctrine of the Trinity, when faced with the Mystery or Runa of whatever is out there, we often need a number of masks for our gods to wear.

As to the "why?" we do this, I'm sure there are a whole range of reasons, but for brevity's sake I will touch briefly on two:

Firstly, the allowance for multiplicity allows us to make sense of new experiences of the numinous that disrupt our current worldviews. For the first century Jewish community trying to make sense of their encounter with Jesus, there was an inevitable struggle as they sought to harmonize their experience of the risen Christ with their existing monotheism – was this being a God? Should we address our perceived messiah as "Lord"? Certainly we can see the evolution of competing interpretations as the church evolved its thinking in the centuries prior to the Nicene creed (for those interested in this check out "Christology in the Making" by James Dunn). Multiplicity allows us to 'upload' new insights and experiences into our perception of the numinous.

As a Gnostic explorer travelling my path, I am aware of my own process of canonisation as I promote and demote incoming ideas and insights within my personal pantheon. While a degree of narcissism is somewhat inevitable for the magician, ideally this process is one of slow evolution rather than merely being brash consumerism. In the pursuit of depth in my relationship with god-forms, I cast a spell on myself as their faces are reflected in my art, relationships and the altars I make.

Secondly, I think that many of us seek models of divine multiplicity because they more accurately reflect our experience of self. As human beings trying to make sense of our universe, we have to deal with a whole host of competing desires and demands as we try and prioritise the needs of individual, family and tribe. These competing and sometimes conflicting needs then become translated into self-states that we oscillate between, dependent on a complex mash-up of genes, conditioning and personality structure. To experience such tensions seems to be an inevitable part of the human condition and it is perhaps unsurprising that we seek spiritual myths and metaphors that make sense of them.

My own interest in weird cosmologies like that of the Process and the early Gnostics is that the maps that they were working with seem to have a more creative engagement with both darkness and dynamic tension. Unlike the rather safe stylings of a Father, Son and Holy Spirit who are rarely at odds with each other, the various players of the Gnostic stage often represent stages of unfolding, and the resolution of various core conflicts. It was hardly surprising that as Jung sought to evolve his model of depth psychology, he found so much of interest in these strange waters. Such rich mythic multiplicities steer us away from the shallows of safe 'belief' and ask that we push out into the depths of the unknown.

Space; the Final Frontier

One of my earliest spiritual experiences was one in which I became clearly aware of my smallness in the Universe. As a fledgling meditator of 12 years of age I 'panned back' in my mind's eye to take in my room, my street, and my country until I felt as though I was looking down on a distant blue ball suspended in the dark vastness of space.

I was recently reminded of this experience as I watched Neil deGrasse Tyson describing the unfolding story of the Universe's development. In listening to his wonderful reworking of Carl Sagan's "Cosmos", I was left awestruck at the scale of the Universe both in terms of its expanding dimensions and the relative brevity of human evolution when mapped against known time.

As I gaze out at the night sky, I find myself unable to find lasting meaning in any prevailing Metaphysical position, be it a theistic one or that of the strict rationalist. The mystery and expansiveness of space seems to empty me of the trite and obvious. My sense of awe seems to both induce a sense of mild panic as I glimpse the limits of my control and understanding, while at the same time beckoning me onwards into the depths of the unknown.

While I personally find little of value in the astrological preoccupations of many ancient civilisations, I can appreciate the sense of power and significance that they attributed to the movement of heavenly bodies against the silent blackness of the night sky. In the midst of life's busyness and apparent chaos, the steady track of the stars told us stories of an ongoing struggle and cosmic return.

As an expression of our humanity, the occult sciences have attributed an almost endless array of complicating correspondences. Whether the planets become gnostic archons, or we are trying to glean the significance of "Saturn being in Taurus", in our attempts to invest meaning and divine causation we may be in danger of producing even more cognitive clutter.

If we can set aside our constructs and schemas in order to embrace a Zen-like "beginner's mind" what might we find ourselves encountering? Far be it from me to dictate your experience, but in gazing at the darkness of Space, I continue to experience a sense of vastness, transcendence and terror!

In grappling with the limitations of what we can perceive, we cannot help being moved by vastness. Concepts and control are threatened by the limitations of our knowledge and the sense of mystery that Space seems to hold.

Often our longing to explore these realms mirrors the initiatory drive to create and explore a greater sense of spaciousness within ourselves. Such exploration has been a key part of my own spiritual journey, and the rationale for integrating Zen sitting into our Hearth meetings has been to allow our entry into such expansive realms. The integration of such apparently disparate pagan and Buddhist inflected perspectives aims to enable us to both embrace the Self while acknowledging the benefits of loosening our hold on certainty.

Gazing upwards at the Cosmos, at that which appears spatially "up" and beyond our lives in all their messiness, our creative engagement with Space can also fuel our longing for the transcendent. In both Ken Wilber's integral teachings and Gurdjieff's neo-hermeticism, the Cosmic (or Kosmic) represents a move away from the temporary material realm and toward the unified and eternal. Personally speaking, while I tend not to buy into dualism, such spatial metaphors can provide us with potent psychological tools for triggering personal transformation. The sense of otherness and potentiality that the Cosmic 'up' can represent, need not be a move away from our Earth and our bodies, but it can act as a catalyst in driving us on toward those hopes or aspirations that currently feel so distant. Cosmos contains within its spaces the chaotic potentiality of the void; as we shape this dark matter through the skillful application of will, so strange new things become possible.

While my star-gazing has thus far has sounded quite chirpy, it can also be terror-filled. To experience a sense of our smallness and brevity can trigger all sorts of existential despair. No one ever promised that the process of waking up was either easy or pain-free. Unsurprisingly, I am not the first gnostic explorer to make such observations and one could hardly imagine a chaos current without the horror filled vision of Howard Philips Lovecraft.

For me the world of Lovecraft embodies our sense of terror in response to the Universe's vastness and uncertainty. The monster-gods of the mythos – Azathoth, Nyarlathotep et al – provide us with a potent set of shadow archetypes that give form to our profound sense of dis-ease. On one level the Mythos seems to have little sense of comfort or redemption, but I wonder whether they, like wrathful Buddha-forms, can be sat with and glanced at sideways. By naming our terrors and giving them shape, arguably we accomplish some degree of containment. They may well still lurk in the stygian depths or between the blackness between the stars, but giving them form may make them (slightly) more manageable.

The vastness of Space invites us to both wonder and explore. Despite the fear that we might experience, its allure and mystery call forth the adventurer within that we might "boldly go where no one has gone before....".

As those awesome doom metallers Neurosis have observed:
"Recognise this as your own nature
Abandon the fear
Abandon the terror you project
Let your mind rest beyond flesh and bone
Look from a place of understanding
Your mind is a conduit
Your mind is as vast as the universe
Rest in this

A Gnostic's Progress
  In the clear light of existence
  This light is divine."

  "Prayer" from the Sovereign E.P.

Conversations with a Cosmonaut

In my own explorations of Gnosis, one of my friends whose work I have found consistently inspiring has been Dr. Lloyd Keane. What follows is an interview that Lloyd graciously agreed to with regards to his own initiatory work:

1. Could you tell us a little about your own magical background? (How you got into it.)

I hate this question. Answering it brings up some pretty embarrassing moments and yet those moments lead me to where I am now so it can't be all bad. Still... ugh.

My magical background began with three books: *The Black Arts* by Cavendish, *Modern Magic* by Kraig, and *Wicca: A Guide for the Solitary Practitioner* by Cunningham. At that early time I was also a member of A.M.O.R.C. So basically I was a very sincere and dedicated White Lighter. Theological thrillers such as *The Omen*, *The Exorcist*, and *The Prince of Darkness* inspired me too. And of course *Star Wars* was a huge influence! I would have to say it was the notion of forbidden and really super-real knowledge symbolized (and commodified) by all the books in the local occult shop at the time that really dragged me in. My journals from that time are remarkably naive and yet utterly sincere. I have been practicing some form of "magical" tradition since roughly 1987-88.

Lloyd's altar

2. You've worked in a few different traditions, could you tell us about those and your current affiliations?

Well as my answer to your first question clearly indicates I was setting myself up for all manner of problems. In a strange way Wicca provided me with an emotional outlet for my ceremonial/ritual magic, and the ceremonial/ritual magic provided me with intellectual curiosities like Kabbala and alchemy. Really they both reflected my yearning for Mystery. Later I developed a deep love for Crowley's writings and Thelema (or rather, my mystical non-threatening, non-orgy, non-recreational drug version of Thelema) as well as a connection to Irish pagan revival and Asatru (or rather, my mystical non-believing, non-kindred, giant-loving version of Asatru). Again, Crowley's Nuit as well as Odin and the Etins all reflected Mystery and vastness. Off the top of my head I've been a member of A.M.O.R.C., two online Golden Dawn groups, B.O.T.A., an associate member of the OTO, a Probationer in a lineage of the A∴A∴, the Troth, and the Rune Gild. I also worked closely with a friend and mentor in Wicca for at least ten years. In some ways this reflects a haphazard approach to Initiation, and in another way it demonstrates my systematic search for something that I could not find from any of these organizations and traditions.

One day something snapped in me. Something had changed. I was going to leave an offering to Thor (Odin was far too spooky) and I thought to myself "This is it? This is what I'll be doing when I'm 80!?" I was in an existential crisis and two websites grabbed me by the throat: the Church of Satan and the Temple of Set. I loved the ridiculously and seriously playful aesthetic of the Church of Satan. It was so different from anything else I experienced up to that point. However, the Temple of Set website was, at the time, this strange blue colour. It had an inverse pentagram (or a properly proportioned pentagon... however you want to see it), and the monolith from 2001. Top that off with a quote from Plato and I was utterly confused and fascinated. There was something *deep* in that imagery.

After much hesitation (and rewriting my application) I applied to join the Temple of Set and I've been a member since then. I'm currently a Priest of Set, a Master in the Esoteric Order of Beelzebub, and a member of the Order of Tiamat.

3. Much of your current practice makes use of visual art and music; can you describe some of these explorations and why you find these methods so helpful?

That's a really good question. I've always been a doodler and I've always played around with artistic creation. However my work in the Temple of Set helped me focus my understanding and use of art as an Initiatory tool and form of expression. One of the things that makes the human animal unique (as far as we can tell) is the drive to create. We create things that have no overt, ontological, purpose. This drive to create is stimulated by what we could call the Black Flame. Taking that metaphor, this substance, this flame of isolate intelligence, can (and I would say *should*) be applied to creating Initiatory works of art (of whatever form or format). I also strive to inspire others to connect with and work with that Flame. I may not be technically advanced in my art but I often communicate and transmit my meaning very well. It can become entertainingly annoying when highly talented artists email me to say that something I created inspired them to begin creating again. Great. So glad I could be of service, now go create something that I could never create in a million years. At least that inspires me to keep going. My music is the same thing. I *must* create. I go squirrely if I'm not drawing or manipulating images, or playing music. Often creating things helps me work through ideas or issues I'm dealing with as part of Initiation (for me Initiation and living one's life are synonyms). I am able to understand or approach Initiatory issues from various angles by creating something concrete from the stirrings of subjective inspiration.

4. Many of your explorations touch on themes around depth, vastness and awe. Could you tell us why such themes are important in your own initiatory work?

I think all those aspects are part of Mystery or *Runa*. At least, on one level I think that it's part of it. Mystery has been with me from a very early time. However, often my experience of Mystery was filtered through other people's interpretations. I was told Mystery was a God(s)dess(es), Angel, HGA, ancestors... everything *except* what resonated with *me*. Depth, vastness, and awe are core facets of the experience of the numinous, and that experience of the

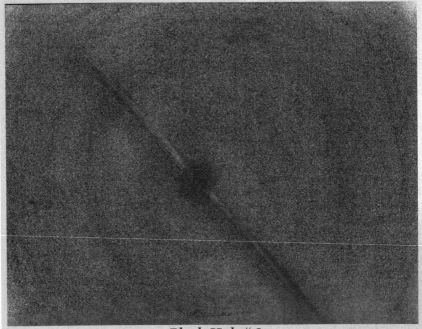

Black Hole #2

numinous is another way of describing the experience of Mystery (keeping in mind that there are varying degrees of the experience of the numinous). Another important facet of such themes is that they help to act as a cosmic eliminator of occultnik douchebaggery. I get so tired of people saying how they are living gods (or demons or angels), or how their HGA is uber divine, or that they are an incarnation of Crowley. Just sit still for a moment. Contemplate how vast our solar system is. Then think of how utterly miniscule it is from the perspective of the nearest supermassive black hole. Really in the grand scheme of things we are pretty insignificant. I have found that encouraging that sense of awe and dread is a good way to reset my own hubris. Not that I have such problems. Obviously I'm beyond such pettiness.

5. How do these ideas connect to your work within the Esoteric Order of Beelzebub?

Actually it's interesting, I find that my work within the Esoteric Order of Beelzebub (EOB) and within the Order of Tiamat both reflect the ideas of vastness and awe in different ways. For me EOB is about exploring the Black Flame. It is about engaging with substance, energy, and purposefulness and it is about cultivating independence, inspiration, and invention. In this case the deepness and awe comes from experiencing ourselves, who we really are when we are free from what other people have told us we are and are not. EOB uses the term "Cosmonaut" to refer to its members. This is a playful title, but it is also very poignant. We are explorers. We want to wander out into the vast expanse of our being and see what we can discover and we bring that knowledge back to share with our fellow explorers. Well at least that's this Cosmonaut's perspective!

The Order of Tiamat approaches deepness and awe through dread. In this case we can see Tiamat, mother of the eleven monsters, mother of the Abyss, as something so utterly beyond comprehension as to lead to existential dread. Lovecraft very much captured this idea of dread. The Mesopotamians had a word for it: *Melammu.* This is the sense of the numinous that their gods were said to exude. By working with this sense of awe we can come to integrate it into our own Being.

The exploration of vastness, and the full awareness of our place in the cosmos, alternate throughout my art and my approach to Initiation.

6. Many people view the god Set as having strong stellar/cosmic connections, can I ask how such links are important in your own magical work?

This is a difficult question. I don't work much with how the ancient Egyptians apprehended Set. There is a great deal of evidence linking Set with stars and stellar traditions. I guess I approach this aesthetically or metaphorically. The stellar roots of Setian thought are distinct from say, Thelema or witchcraft or Wicca, for example. With Thelemic religion we have the solar phallic, in your face, Ra-Hoor. In Wicca, at least a good number of traditions within Wicca, there is an emphasis on the moon, the Earth Mother, the Goddess. Set has warlike aspects of a solar god but Set is far more alien and *unnatural.* Again metaphorically speaking, Set is not bound to an earth or lunar perspective. Set is not bound to a solar perspective. Set dwells behind the Constellation of the Thigh (Big Dipper). Set's playground is the deep vastness of space.

Sowilo

I often think of this wonderful quote from *The Stars my Destination*:

"*Gully Foyle is my name*
And Terra is my nation.
Deep space is my dwelling place,
The stars my destination."

To me this quote summarises my work as a Cosmonaut and as a Setian.

7. What direction do you see your initiatory work heading in the future?

Another great question. Thank you.

I'm actively working to refine and articulate my own approach to Setian Initiation. This is a difficult though necessary task and it is just beginning. This process will have a major impact on my art and my understanding of awe, deepness, and Mystery. What that will look like in the end I can't say for sure. For now it is in the Yet to Be and when I get there I will let you know!

What I Find Myself Doing...

Having spent time thinking about the various ways in which the Gnostic material can impact upon contemporary spiritual paths, it seems only right that I reflect upon the way in which this is manifested in my own religious life. Having spent half this short book considering the Gnostics and what their message means for us, it seems sensible to reflect on the specifically Chaos-Pagan inspired shaped form that my own Gnostic experiments have taken.

As someone who has spent over 30 years exploring the variety of religious answers devised by humanity's attempt to make sense of life on our planet, it got me thinking about the "Why Odin?" question. What is it about his mythological heroism that I find so compelling? Why with my own pointy-hatted chaos magickal ways do I keeping coming back to his story as an exemplar of how to manage my own existential dilemmas?

Some critics of the neo-pagan revival typify its worldview as a naive pantheism where the preoccupation with the cycle of Nature prevents us from appreciation of the evolutionary goal of transcendence (see the work of Ken Wilber for more on this). In reality, heathen myths are not some distant utopian vision or romantic aspiration to "be at one with nature". Rather they seem to mirror the joy and struggle of our own human experience. The stories that fill both the Eddas and Sagas represent a complex interlacing of history and pre-history as an expression of an ever shifting, ever evolving world. While we may take pleasure in the making of toasts and the wearing of skins, I personally feel that the ancestors would have a good belly laugh at attempts to recapture some imagined "golden-age"!

When we examine Heathen cosmology, unsurprisingly it seeks to mirror the experience of the people of the North as they lived their lives. In the beginning was the primal void (Ginnungagap) and from it emerged the primary polarity of Fire and Ice. From the dynamic tension between these poles came melt-water, and from this emerged the primal giant Ymir. Creation is not a peaceable realm, but one that is forever caught up in a cycle of war and temporary resolution. These tensions are personified by the giants, other elemental beings and the gods themselves, both Aesir and Vanir.

The mythological struggle between Aesir and Vanir (as described in Voluspa and elsewhere) seem to reflect at a macrocosmic level the human project of seeking to awaken consciousness within our bodies and the biosphere. This balancing of immanent and transcendent is also reflected in Odin's own journey. His need to learn magic from Freya highlights the essential journey into the natural so as to comprehend his life and magic, but this is not enough. He must go deeper and seek Runa – the mysteries of Kosmos – via his ordeal on the world tree:

I know that I hung on a windy tree
nine long nights,

wounded by a spear, dedicated to Odin,
myself to myself,
on that tree of which no man knows
from where its roots run.
No bread did they give me or drink from a horn,
Downwards I peered;
I took up the runes, screaming I took them,
Then I fell back from there.

Havamal 138-139

The dimensions of gnosis that he attains are both deep and transcendent (ah, the limits of spatial metaphors!). The mysteries arise from the dark roots of the unconscious (both collective and individual) and they point us towards the reality that the northern Gnostic must awaken within the realm of Midgard. Whichever version of the futhark that we work with, they represent the worldview of the ancestors both in relation to their core values and day-to-day concerns. Like the "Sly Man" of the Gurdjieff Work, for those of us seeking to emulate the path of the All-Father, our awakening needs to integrate and balance the needs of body, mind and emotions. It needs to be here and now rather than in some imagined nirvana/Valhalla.

In contrast to the Gnostic explorers of the classical period, the Northern Gnostic seeks the way of awakening within and through the natural world rather than away from it. This is a path of integration typified by the hermetic axiom of "as above so below, as below so above". We need to wake up from the sleep that culture and routine can lull us into, but our awakening is also a realization of connection and relationship rather than lofty isolation. This is not an easy journey to make; we need to work hard to uncover these often overgrown pathways. Awakening to Runa often brings a greater sense of being out of step with the mainstream – Odin took up the Runes of realization screaming and roaring. As we seek to dive deep into new realms of understanding, we need to understand their true cost: that they can only be accessed when we give up what we think we know to gain true insight – "sacrificing self to self". Here we find ourselves contending with the insights of C.G. Jung and other transpersonal psychological approaches where the ego is not abolished but rather is transformed via expansion and extension to incorporate the dark roots of the unconscious (Hel) and the bright potentialities of what we might become (Asgard).

Runes as Koans

Often people associate quiet and silence as being passive states – often rightly so, but sometimes our silence can take a more active, wondering and exploratory quality.

As we come together to practice, the runes become a tool via which we seek to engage with the mystery of our life in the realm of Midgard. Life can be joyful, painful, meaningful or bewildering and these states are reflected in the Rune rows. When Odin took up the runes he did so roaring and screaming – to seek to grasp the fullness of life's mystery is not the easiest of undertakings.

Much has been made of the difficulty of interpreting the runes, and the danger of imposing one's existing world view or esoteric preoccupations. One of the primary sources of inspiration has understandably been the various rune poems in their Old Norse, Anglo-Saxon and Icelandic forms. Yet, however helpful the rune poems are in helping us interpret the mysteries, I'm guessing I'm not alone in finding them highly enigmatic! Now of course greater application in understanding the linguistic, cultural and historical contexts will undoubtedly bring greater insight, but I still find power in also using a more non-linear approach.

The runes seem to represent at an almost archetypal level the values and concerns of our ancestors. They are the mysterious and elegant summary of their drives and hopes. On one level they can be understood as Cattle, Fire, Transport etc but more deeply they are Runa-Mysteries. As we seek to live our lives and listen to competing demands of work, family and leisure, the runes continue to exert their force and ask us to become something more. For the Zen Odinist they act as koans that challenge our attempts to live tidy, knowable lives – the memetic dynamite of the Gods aiding the process of the awakening for which we secretly long.

Within most Zen traditions koans play an important role in helping loosen the student's hold on linearity. These teaching sayings are sat with and worked with until their presence, like the expansion of water freezing, cracks open consciousness. Like the rune poems, koans are not meaningless riddles, rather they are tools whose potency can only truly be accessed through letting go of our left-brained attempts to problem solve.

In the Zen Hearth of Odin the Wanderer, this awakening within the turning of the year is the focus of our work. Via the use of Zen sitting practice, Runic Galdar and core shamanic trance technologies (i.e. drumming) we seek the wisdom of the old ways so that we might live more fully today. I'll conclude with the statement of intent that we are currently using at our monthly blots:

We come seeking gnosis
And the wisdom to apply it.
We come seeking the Old Ways
That we might truly live now
And become the future.

We come seeking the three realms
And the three treasures
Sky, Earth and Sea
Aesir, Vanir and the Ancestors.
We seek the World Tree as the realm of practice:
Our Minds, our Bodies, our Lives.
We seek to take up the Runes
Fragments of mystery
As we see sense and nonsense
On the road we travel.
We give thanks to the heroes of practice
We give thanks for the complex Web of Truth
We give thanks to those who sit like mountains together.

Gnostic Fan Fiction

I must confess to being excited about some writing that I have had included in a forthcoming anthology. *No Safewords 2* is a collection of short-story fan fiction inspired by the work of Laura Antoniou. For the uninitiated, Laura Antoniou is undoubtedly amongst the world's most talented authors of erotic fiction. In her *Marketplace* series, Laura has created an engaging universe in which beautifully crafted characters explore the world of consensual BDSM (Bondage, discipline and Sadomasochism). While this sexual style may not be everyone's cup of tea, I would highly recommend the six books currently available, as they touch on deep themes about belonging, identity, vocation and of course the nature of passion.

Fan fiction can take a whole plethora of forms, but at its core is a desire to produce new writing or art inspired by an existing canon of work. While it is likely that Fan Fiction as a contemporary phenomenon began as a response to the Kirk/Spock relationship in Star Trek, you can find forms of it that are connected to pretty much any series that engenders significant levels of devotion. This issue of devotion feels important in that the content of a given series is felt to be important enough to inspire the new author to take their heroes' story arc in a new direction.

Famously the Kirk/Spock relationship was central in birthing "Slash" fiction where our protagonists are imagined in a whole range of male-on-male erotic activity, but fan fiction can also take our beloved characters into a whole array of other possible situations. In keeping with its ironic and postmodern nature the series "Sherlock" has generated huge amounts of fan fiction (including some great Sherlock/Watson Slash) while being itself a form of Fan Fiction inspired by Arthur Conan Doyle's original genius. Sherlock reimagines the Conan Doyle characters in 21st century London, but also accentuates aspects of their characters so as to contend with more contemporary concerns. One excellent example of this is the way that Benedict Cumberbatch's depiction of Holmes has been viewed as iconic by people identifying as being on the asexual spectrum. While Conan Doyle's Holmes had decidedly asexual traits, the evolution of Holmes in the Sherlock series has made this more overt and positive depiction of even greater importance.

In my own experience of writing fan fiction (and I don't find fiction the easiest thing to write), my own efforts were probably successful because of my love of the original *Marketplace* series and the degree to which I had soaked myself in the canon that Laura and others have created. Great art often inspires both obsession and inspiration. Perhaps due to our desire to connect to a modern (or postmodern) form of mythology, we look to the hyperreality of the screen and print as a way of making sense of our lives. While the slightly musty myths of the past may feel harder to access, it maybe that the power of story still provides us with an evocative way of touching the deepest aspects of our personal and collective psychologies. This is certainly the case with the Star Wars films and most of us are well aware of the degree to which George Lucas was influenced by Joseph Campbell's work in trying to understand common mythic themes.

Personally I think that fan fiction is awesome. Yes, it can be a decidedly mixed bag in terms of quality, but for me it reflects something brilliant about how we as humans respond to stories that touch us and use the power of these myths to empower our own journeys. The original author may well be horrified by the quality of our art or what we have imagined their characters getting up to, but for me it reflects the tendril-like nature of inspiration that threatens to break apart any attempt to erect walls around a holy canon of work.

In many ways the Gnostics were the original purveyors of fan fiction. While the orthodox elements of the early church were trying to ensure certainty about what Jesus and the apostles did and didn't say, the Gnostics just kept being inspired. It could be argued that even the canonical Gospels of the New Testament (especially John) are perhaps some of the greatest pieces of fan fiction known to history. Whatever one makes of the historicity of Jesus Christ, the idea of his life and mission were hugely inspiring and generated an avalanche of literary responses.

For those with an interest in trying to prevent heresy and innovation, the Gnostic approach to hermeneutics was highly disconcerting. The God of the Old Testament was generally viewed as an inadequate megalomaniac and as for Jesus; well

140

frankly he just wouldn't shut up. While his earliest core sayings may have been brilliant, his inspiration kept igniting the imaginations of those not content with the answers of orthodoxy. While holding a position of profound respect for both Christ and his Apostles, the inspirational torrent of the Nag Hammadi library represents a form of innovation and adaptation that is in keeping with the best of fan fiction.

Those of us who love and produce fan fiction would rarely claim to have reached the levels of creative genius that are present in the primary texts that inspire us. For me fan fiction entails a process of playful investigation as to how these heroic figures of art can fuel my own development and creativity. Imitation can be the greatest form of flattery and also an expression of gratitude for how the great work of others make our lives more doable.

Exercise 4: Writing Your Own Gospel...

In my last chapter about fan fiction I got to wondering about how great works of art can trigger our own process of inspiration. Any material that stirs something deep within us can catalyse our own creative juices in a manner that leads us to express our own creativity into the world of manifestation. The nature of what moves us can be as diverse as the new series of the *X-files* or the *Tao Te Ching*.

We also considered the way in which the Gnostics of the early church could be seen as generating their own fan fiction in response to the life of Jesus and his followers. In contrast to orthodox attempts to delineate 'truth' within a recognised canon of scripture, the Gnostics often viewed the boundaries as far more permeable. If the incoming of gnosis was available to Jesus and his apostles why limit such inspiration? He keeps speaking to us and through producing new Gospels we encounter new challenges and evolve deepened understanding.

In this exercise I'd like you to consider an existing source of personal inspiration that can help you generate your own fan fictional gospel or "Good News". For this fan fiction to be truly good news it must open up for you a greater possibility of freedom and liberation from something that you feel is limiting to you; in gnostic terms we might define these as being archonic. For our art to have gospel force, it must offer us a potential key to a greater sense of "peace, freedom and happiness" (as we say in the Nath tradition).

In my view the best fan fiction tends to be generated by those who are deeply moved by the original source material and have spent time soaking in the canon of that work. From an overtly spiritual perspective, the practice of Lectio Divina (divine reading) offers a number of interesting methods for deepening our engagement with material that we experience as being sacred. Lectio Divina identifies a number of stages that the aspirant or fan might go through in order to further internalise something so as to transform themselves.

In this exercise I'm proposing that we utilise each of these steps in engaging with material of your choice e.g. *Principia Discordia*, *Bhagavad Gita*, the script from *True Detective* (series one!) and then to take this one step further so as to create your own liberating art work.

Stage 1 — Lectio (Reading): Here we read or engage with our primary material in a deliberate, conscious manner. You may want to break it down into small chunks like a couple of verses or a specific scene within a film. I often find reading a text aloud can give it a different voice and provide new insight. If nothing else the reading of something aloud vibrates it through our bodies.

Stage2 — Meditatio (Meditation): During this stage we are reflecting upon or pondering what we have engaged with. In some senses we are seeking a Zen-like beginner's mind, where we try to let go of our assumptions and perhaps the previous meanings we have attached to it. There is perhaps also a sense of slow simmering or percolation as we let the text speak to the varying aspects of our being.

Stage 3 — Oratio (Prayer): This might be a spontaneous prayer response directed towards a deity or we might view it as the bubbling up of our inspired response to our meditations. As we simmer in contemplation so the deeper aspects of ourselves vibrate in response. Such responses should be neither censored nor scripted; rather they reveal something real and unguarded about how something impacts upon us.

Stage 4 — Contemplatio (Contemplation): Here we rest and reflect on the impact of our inspired response. Rather than a fevered response at the height of ecstasy, now we sit with our own process of transformation so as to allow a further maturation of any gnosis gained.

Okay, so far so good! Hopefully you can appreciate how this approach might profoundly enrich and personalise your experience of your chosen form of inspiration. What I'd like to propose for the purposes of this exercise is that we move this method on one stage further in engaging in a further act of creation...

Stage 5 — Creatio (Creation): Having read, meditated and been inspired we are now able to channel this response into our own creative activity. In seeking to work with those archonic forces within our lives we can allow our triggered inspiration to explore those potential routes to greater freedom. For some people this may inspire a freedom-text in the style of the original, but we shouldn't be too tied to producing a replica:

"And lo, on the third day Steve decided that he must flee his pressured job and head to the beach more..."

When inspiration takes hold it may be that your approach will be less linear! Your acts of creation may be in making collage, cooking a great meal for friends or having a proper dance around your kitchen. So much of the stuckness that we experience comes from our need to get it right, but like many things in life most of us do better when we are allowed to relax a bit, to be curious and to explore things playfully.

I hope you have fun with this approach and allow yourself the space to explore how the things you love can inspire the creation of your own art. Peace, love and freedom to those willing to respond to their inner Muse!

Mahayana Gnostics: Part 2

While our acts of creation may initially find expression at a personal level, we should remain awake to the need to explore what these new insights might mean at a collective, socio-political level. As magicians it can be easy to get lost within the labyrinthine halls of our dedicated spooky clubs. In seeking to plumb the depths of mystery and our own process of psychological change, we can be endlessly inventive in developing techniques and elaborate symbol systems. While some folks may find value in roaming the paths of the Qliphoth or in liaising with denizens of the Nightside, it seems fair that at some point we should ask ourselves "what difference does that actually make?".

Personally I think that the socio-political implications of our occult explorations will be as diverse and complex as the religions themselves. It may well be that the libertarianism of a Setian, as well as the eco-collectivism of a druid, are equally valid ethical stances generated by their personal philosophies. To me, what feels critical is that our claims to personal development or magical advancement need to birth something that contributes to the betterment of humanity.

This is not to suggest that we all need to be reduced to blanket prescriptions as to the focus and shape that our activism should take. The manifestation of our spiritual passion into the realm of Midgard can take many forms. Whether via writing, music, marching, advocacy or innovative financial investment, the

146

forms of our engagement are rightly tailored to our personal preferences and drives.

In the excellent *All Acts of Love and Pleasure: Inclusive Wicca* (2015) by Yvonne Aburrow we are given a really helpful overview of Wicca's historical development, and the wide variety of theological positions that initiates into that tradition might hold: e.g. forms of monism, duotheism, polytheism and animism. These are rarely neatly delineated positions, and often huge overlaps and apparent inconsistencies appear as people seek to live the reality of how they engage with their experience of the Gods.

Yvonne reflects on the manner in which a Pagan theology might evolve and progress, in reflecting upon and adapting its theology to incorporate social changes. Her work triggered my own reflections as to how my own take on Pagan/occult Theology might help shape my own attempts to evolve a deeper sense of engagement. This list is by no means definitive but I hope it will provide some inspiration for your own reflections:

1. **Multiplicity:** Even if one's Paganism takes a decidedly scientific and monistic form, there is usually an engagement with the concept of Polytheism at a mythic/psychological level. The idea that we should understand the divine as a series of differing beings (or principles) that have an interaction or relationship with each other is appealing for many of us. While Polytheism can take many theological forms, what it does seem to entail is a move towards acknowledging the multiple, the complex, and the

relational nature of how we experience life and contemplate the numinous-what we might call "Pantheonic" consciousness.

In our devotional work we may well chose to focus our energies towards a specific deity within a given pantheon; e.g. the God of consciousness, the female destroyer, the Son of new endeavors etc., but we remain conscious of the whole. Similarly in our activism we may focus on a given issue (indeed we have only so much time and energy) but seek to resist becoming overly narrow in perspective.

In reflecting on this emphasis on theological interconnection, I couldn't help but think about the general increase in awareness of intersectionality with regards both identity and social issues-issues rarely (if ever) stand in isolation, rather the parts affect the whole in a way that demonstrates the subtle ecology of any given situation. Such awareness helps us more fully appreciate not only the weight of multiple struggles but also the positive impact that change in one sphere can have in creating larger scale change.

2. Localised discourse: In my practice, much attention is given to location and what might loosely be called "the spirit of place". As much as my being a magician is located somewhere my head and heart, it only really becomes activated within the context of "what's out there". I can only really focus and shape magical attention when I am in the place of doing it.

In many ways my activism (i.e. living my life in relationship with self and others) is profoundly shaped by the place I find myself in. Yes I am increasingly connected globally, and engaged in struggling to evolve macro scale principles, but "small is beautiful" still has meaning. Yes I may contribute by signing numerous online petitions, but what am I willing to do within my immediate communities? How can I use a form of "social animism" to tune-in to how reflection and change might occur at a grassroots level?

3. Importance of human drives: In her book Yvonne helpfully seeks to examine ideas of what holiness, piety and sacredness might mean for the modern pagan. In contrasting an integrative Wiccan perspective with potentially more dualistic paths, we can begin to evolve ethical and spiritual positions that have sensuality at their core.

While issues such as sexual liberty and artistic expression may be seen as somewhat peripheral when confronted by issues such as poverty, war and terrorism, it is my view that they are often at the very heart of why these conflicts take place. The drives to experience pleasure and to express creativity are central to humanity's attempt to find meaning in life. Many conflicts and the resulting social inequalities seem to result from trying to overly police these passions via either religious or political means. In seeking such constraint and potential suppression, it is sadly all too common that that those threatened by their own humanity then project onto an "Other" who becomes demonised in the process. For our spiritual paths to take seriously the pursuit of sacredness in its fullest sense, it must call us back to the sensual and provide a challenge to thin-lipped piety.

While there are always dangers inherent in the process of seeking to evolve forms of religion that are more inclusive and liberal (consumerism and over-simplicity spring to mind!), it does offer the possibility of informing any unfolding of social change. These are evolutionary processes that rejoice in the way in which our ever-inventive humanity interacts with the divine. To be open about this unfolding does not rob our religions of power; rather, they ask us to seek and use power consciously.

Post-Christian, not Post-Christic

Perhaps it comes as some surprise, given my Christian history, that it has taken me this long to address the thorny issue of that old trouble-maker Yeshua Ben Yosef (Jesus to his Greek speaking friends). This may be partially due to the degree of emotional baggage I still have in relation to him, but also acknowledges the complexity of the scholarly debate around the significance of his life.

Whatever one makes of claims regarding the historical accuracy of the New Testament record, one would be hard pressed to deny the mythic potency of the Jesus story and the seismic impact that responses to it have had on world history. His impact continues to be inescapable both personally and culturally. However revolutionary our freshly minted post-Christian or revived polytheistic world views, the software from the past 2,000 years is still running and even the most thorough-going pagan reconstructionist seems to be responding to it at least unconsciously.

In the hands of monotheism, the myth of the dying and rising god has provided a decidedly mixed bag of outcomes as we humans have tried to make sense of the mystery of existence.

As a result of my own Christian past, the presupposition pool that I swim in is going to be one in which I remain sensitised to motifs within the pagan/magical community that echo Judeo-Christian themes. In seeking to escape the limitations of the

151

sexism, homophobia and speciesism that have often been perceived as going hand-in-hand with Christianity, it seems that many of us have fallen into some seemingly inevitable traps. Whether by idealising paganisms past or failing to see the genuinely helpful spiritual impulses of the Christic tradition, we can all be guilty of developing blind spots as we are temporarily dazzled by the shiny newness of neo-paganism.

My own attraction to the Gnostics and heretics more generally has been their willingness to take risks in re-imagining their personal engagement with the person and myth of Jesus Christ. Theirs is a Christianity that displaces dry orthodoxies with their personalized interpretation of historic teachings and present tense visionary encounters. While I may choose not to adopt the moniker "Christian" because of the weight of past associations that it holds for me, I remain deeply inspired by many who embraced that path.

Given the difficulties that I have had with claims of religious exclusivity during my own journey, I continue to be interested in expressions of Christic gnosis that allow for the rich diversity of manifestations within a more universal vision. The experience of *anointing* or the awakening to new aspects of ourselves can rarely be contained within the clean parameters of control that many faith communities seek to police. While I acknowledge my own bias, for me it is on these blurry edges between things that the most interesting shifts take place.

What I find really interesting, as Neo-paganism enters its third or fourth generations, is the increasingly important role that is being played by those traditions (both new and old) that are making creative use of the meeting points that exist between apparently divergent currents. In the course of mulling over some of these ideas I was struck once again by Isaac Bonewits' ideas regarding "Mesopaganism":

"The term MesoPagan was first put forth by Isaac Bonewits in an attempt to categorize modern Paganism. According to Bonewits, MesoPagan religions are those that developed from PaleoPagan or native Pagan religions that were influenced by Monotheistic, Dualistic or Nontheistic philosophies. These include all synchretic religions including Christo-Paganism, many Afro-Diasporic faiths, such as Voudun, Santeria and Candomble, and Sikhism as well as many occult traditions including Thelema, Freemasonry, Rosicrucianism, Theosophy and Spiritualism and many modern Witchcraft traditions, including many Wiccan denominations. Also, some Satanic traditions could fall into this category.

The definition of MesoPaganism is nearly identical with that of syncretism, a word that enjoys common use in academic circles."

From http://www.witchipedia.com/mesopaganism

Although the term may have limited value in that almost all pagan religious expression seems to have syncretism as one of its defining traits, it does point toward a more transparent recognition of key component parts that are being held together. Practitioners laying claim to 'traditional' witchcrafts or African diaspora lineages seem, in part, to be attracted to the dynamic frisson created when we attempt to hold together ideas and practices that fall outside neat categorization.

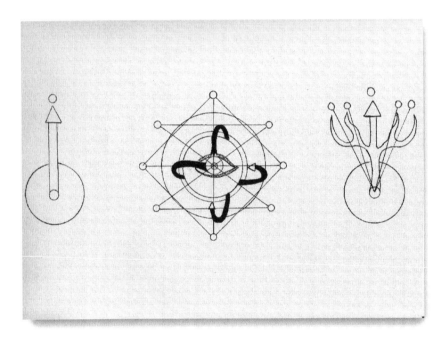

Path #2

This can be challenging terrain to understand, and often we flounder as we attempt to compartmentalize ideas and to formulate our theologies whilst removed from the ritual chamber or circle. To me it feels that the organic symbiosis that exists in these traditions is profoundly praxiological. Yes read books, visit websites etc. but personally I learn more when I see the dissonant array of iconography on an altar space or experiment with technique with some intrepid chums.

On a personal level, the process of syncretism is part of my own journey towards integration. Beyond the labels and brand names of faiths and orders are my own struggles to make sense of the tension between the transcendent and the imminent, sense and nonsense. What does it mean to seek awakening within this world and in this bodymind? Perhaps the tension generated as we wrestle with the dialectic shakes us out of our slumber and takes us to a juncture at which new truths can be found. As someone who is both a Jungian and a guarded optimist, I believe that our struggle to find meaning and to balance the light and shadow of ourselves, will have their evolutionary expression through our art, science and religion, whichever symbol set we personally choose to adopt.

If we journey to the crossroads in our attempt to rediscover our magic, we are inevitably entering a realm of liminal possibility. The crossroads is a meeting place of apparent opposites and seeming contradictions. The dynamic tension generated by the friction between these polarities makes it the place of initiation. In my own journey while it might be easy to view my Christian past as being a time of constriction and repression, the liberating agenda of the Christic myth still seemed to be at work. While my initial flight into Christianity was largely related to my adolescent confusion about my sexuality and gender identity, the Queerness of mystery still broke through via my personal relationship with the figure (historical or otherwise) of Jesus.

While fully recognizing my own projections onto the gospel narrative, I found in my reading of Jesus a blurry Queerness that remains inspiring. In a personal world where maleness, force and certainty made little sense to me, my own gnostic encounter allowed access to a gentler, more mysterious experience. Christ became a mirror via which I could look at myself and come closer to embrace the possibility of who I might become. Such reflection arguably (and perhaps ironically) allowed me to become accepting enough of my self that I no longer wished to call myself a Christian. This Gnostic Christ was asking me to grow up and take some responsibility for my path. The results have not always been tidy or pain-free, but the alternative was to remain coated in the claustrophobic safety of childlike sentimentality.

Art, Altars and the Creation of Gnostic Space

We have already spent much time pondering how themes of duality, distance and tension are present within the gnostic tradition. We have looked at the way in which the discomforts that we experience in the world, both physical and psychological, relate to the tension that seems to exist between our hunger for stillness on the one hand and creative activity on the other. Drawing upon those hermetic and alchemical traditions that place an emphasis on synthesis and return, those of us seeking to pursue a path of magical awakening can take inspiration from their acts of creation, born of dynamic flux. While our instinct for peace may long for a place of resolution, most of us recognize that our truly transformational activity is generated by situations of greater tension/friction.

Thinking of Crowley's formula of Magic(k) being "The Art and Science of causing change in accordance with Will" I tend by temperament to lean towards the art end of things. While I am a big admirer of Pete Carroll's work, when he starts to rattle off the maths of why he thinks magic works I find myself getting a bit sleepy. In contrast to this, my own magic is inspired by the mind-bending energy of abstract expressionism, surrealism and the jagged edges of contemporary performance art.

Whichever medium one chooses (e.g. dance, music, poetry), to do art is to risk an act of creation. While the realm of pure ideas may be one of tidy stillness, to have creation blocked is a death knell to our full humanity. For me art is at its best when it revels in its multiplicity and fuzzy-edged imprecision. In defiance of Academia's attempt to pin down and dissect, the gloriously bloody mess of true performance and expression pushes us into a magically liminal space. To enter such interzones asks that we loosen our hold on what we think we know and who we think we are.

While the best acts of creation ask us to dig deep into the bits of ourselves that often seem most mysterious, elusive and challenging (cf. Lloyd's interview), we also need to direct these energies using the skilled application of our conscious mind. This is the work of the Red Mage, the magician channelling their inner demiurge in holding together nox and lux.

For me, my altar space acts as an anchor point both in my home and my life more generally. While there is a certain degree of order in the way in which I have placed my magical tools and deity statues, I am generally more interested in the more inexact sense of mood which the whole altar represents. My altar is a place where dualities are held and explored, and where the unfolding story of my magical path is sculpted.

Sophia is on my altar as both the primal Mother, and as the Madonna with child. She sits with an icon of Abraxas on her left, and a wooden weather-worn Buddha to her right; her centrality speaks of my current magical obsessions, but more importantly I believe that her wisdom is manifested in the glorious imprecision of my spiritual longings. As with the mythic Sophia mediating between the still realm of the Pleroma and the messy creativity of the Demiurge, so divine wisdom allows us to work with the dynamics of duality that we experience in our lives. This isn't an easy fix or premature synthesis of polarities, rather it often involves a prolonged sitting with, and acknowledging, our own sense of uncertainty.

The altar in my experience provides a liminal zone in which the magician is able to soak-in a more impressionistic sense of their personal Great Work. This is a form of magic that by the very subtlety of its nature is difficult to articulate and needs to be subject to ongoing revision. This is magic that for me is strongly related to Heidegger's idea of mood, and it is virtually impossible to articulate its potency without a personal immersion in the flow of its experience.

This has many similarities to the observations that Ariel Glucklich has captured in his study of magical practitioners in Banaras: for us to begin to grasp the idea of 'magical consciousness', we need to understand that magic is both relational (between practitioner and client) and it takes place in a liminal state of consciousness. Within such states of being the micro-analysis of linear causation is suspended and there is a recognition that a different set of parameters are at play. If we try to understand our own experience of the magical process outside such an enlivened, weirdly infused discourse, it seems likely that comprehension will be more limited.

What I'm trying to point towards, is that in my gnostic explorations, the dynamics of fluctuating creativity (Abraxas) and divine wisdom (Sophia) are not only manifested by the iconography that I have incorporated in my altar space, but also that they are present as guiding principles within the entire magical process that my altar space represents.

Curiosity and Gnostic Uncertainty

For me the themes of awe, depth and vastness that Lloyd touched upon in his interview, are vital to understanding the relevance of the Gnostic message for today. While the vital immanence of the natural world provides much to inspire reverence and to drive magical work, the alien, the distant and cosmic also have much to offer.

The Pleroma dwells in the depth of mystery, the divine emptiness that represents an expansive depth of consciousness that description struggles to approach. It seems somewhat obvious, but as we humans contemplate the vastness of the night sky and the movement of mysterious heavenly bodies, it makes sense that we locate the distant God of still perfection 'out there'. Astrophysics may have opened up a small window in understanding these depths of mystery or Runa, but one cannot help but be laid bare by Space's awe inducing vistas.

This sense of wonder and curiosity has to lie at the beginning of any initiatory process. Whether it's a sense of amazement at the natural order (both Terran and Cosmic) or a profound unease at the simplistic explanations handed down by authorities, these things trigger a process of curious questioning. In my view it is often the internal tension produced by such questioning that can trigger Gnostic insight.

In my day job as a psychological therapist I am often asked (for both myself and my clients) to both promote curiosity and to sit with uncertainty. In grappling with how to do this more effectively, I was struck by some of the great insights provided by the systemic psychotherapist Barry Mason. In his own work with families he sought to ask: "is uncertainty mainly a path to creativity or a path to paralysis?"

In pondering this question, he outlines three types of knowing: unsafe certainty (based on outdated or inaccurate assumptions), unsafe uncertainty (one's environment provides neither safety nor coherent beliefs) and finally safe uncertainty. Safe uncertainty exists when one's environment and strategies for managing life allows for uncertainty to be lived with and even embraced.

Now I like this a lot – in my own journey I have experienced faith based certainty which gave a period of respite. For me it provided a warm fog that 'protected' me from much of life's sharpness. As I have previously, I felt a genuine grief when I had to walk away from certainties that were no longer congruent with my experience of reality. My certainty was no longer safe.

Mason talks about the need to cultivate curiosity and seeks to frame the therapist's role as being one of an explorer who seeks to embody "authoritative doubt". Such a description seems highly applicable for those of us seeking the Magi's path.

Magicians are generally those interested in exploring the terrain of the psyche and body rather than rushing toward union with the divine. Curiosity, experimentation and reflection create an interactive process where the Self becomes a lab from which working hypotheses can be derived and refined. Such reflective experiments can be wide in their parameters and address the big issues such as our sex lives, the food that we eat, and what we think about death.

I have to confess, my problem with 'believing' in things has followed me on my journey. I am a half-hearted Thelemite and a piss-poor pagan, but perhaps this allows me to be a moderately effective Gnostic! Crowley both annoys and inspires me and I find that most polytheistic pantheons fail to hold my attention. What I have always been drawn to are those outsider Gods of consciousness. These are the Magician Gods, that embody the archetype of the individual who is seeking to awaken and explore. Shiva, Odin, Set, Sekhmet, Mercury – truth seekers who themselves are wrestling with the mysteries of the universe. Wisdom and power are hard won for these Gods – eyes are sacrificed, brothers are killed, and periods of celibacy are embraced. It's this type of consciousness or awareness that I am seeking.

Perhaps it seems somewhat ironic to be talking in the same breath of both Gnosis and not-knowing, but arguably some of our best insights are generated when we stop creating more speculative clutter and start a process of deep, attentive listening.

The focus on becoming, and the discovery of Will, has not been an act of teeth gritting and über-humanity; rather one of my primary goals has also been the cultivation of receptivity. In pursuit of liberating praxis and the expression of existential bravery, I have noticed that my directed intent seems more effective when it is less about an attempt to enforce will, and more an exercise in observing where the fault lines of probability are and then enhancing them.

In seeking to manage my uncertainty and the fear of not being able to control all and comprehend all, I can still choose to act. Paradoxically this also entails the action of non-action i.e. sitting with and accepting mystery and the limits of what can be currently known. My own personal praxis centers on the use of approaches that at once develop Will and also help me to sit with mystery and not knowing. Thankfully moments of Gnosis do break through, but Wisdom advises that however startling such insights might intially seem, they are still partial in nature.

Our Gnosis must not allow false comfort, rather it should (at least this side of death) provide a catalyst to greater curiosity and exploration. To see, even if "through a glass darkly" is to be troubled and to acknowledge the desire for something deeper. Something more is a beginning.

A Call to Abraxas

A lot of space in this book has been given over to the way in which magical explorers tend to engage with the world. While ideas and abstract metaphysical concepts are hugely important in shaping the way we experience the universe, they are treated as a hypothesis that the magician tests and refines rather than a received truth.

While the archetypal image of the mage may conjure images of pointy hatted persons seeking to cajole the universe via the force of their will, this need not always be the case. Through reading this work I hope you have been able to gain some insights into a more listening orientated, receptive form of magical practice.

This magic can be both gentle and violent. We listen to the whispers of the still, small voice and are thrown to the ground in possession states. When we take the risk of looking deep into the Well of Wyrd, we bring back oracular fragments that change both speaker and hearer. Whichever strange or alien god puts a call upon our life, these are visions forced through the body; a gnosis whose internal tension triggers transformation. Such tension causes discomfort and with discomfort change.

With this experimental perspective in mind I thought it would be fitting to conclude with a piece of poetry that was an outflowing generated by my own explorations of the Gnostic current:

I call to you O dweller on the knife-edge,

Ambidextrous God,

Both hands, both paths:

A Shadow God, in the half-light of the pre-dawn,

Cockerel headed,

Rooting us in darkness and showing us the Sun.

Skirting Mysteries as Serpent legs

Move in and out of sight.

Creator, destroyer, begettor, purveyor of half-truths

That hold Wisdom still.

I think I know you,

And as I breathe in,

A Serpent tightens-

Wrapped thrice point five around my spine.

Breathing out

Silent Sophia beckons:

A deeper night, whose threshold you safeguard.

Hail to thee O great Abraxas

Whose glorious horror haunts me still!

Bibliography

Assagioli, R. (1990) *Psychosynthesis* Northamptonshire: Crucible

Bateson, G. (1973) *Steps to an Ecology of Mind* London: Granada

Brekke, D. (2010) *The Gnostics* Harvard: First Harvard University Press

Carroll, P. (1987) *Liber Null and Psychonaut* Boston: Weiser

Carroll, P. (1992) *Liber Kaos* Boston: Weiser

Cohn, N. (1975) *Europe's Inner Demons* Sussex: Sussex University Press

Csikszentmihalyi, M. (2002) *Flow* London: Rider

Curton, T.(1997) *The Gnostics* New York: Barner and Noble Press

Dunn, J. (1980) *Christology in the Making* Norwich: SCM

Ehrman, B. (2003) *Lost Scriptures* Oxford: Oxford University Press

Epperly, B. (2011) *Process Theology: A Guide for the Perplexed* London: T&T Clark International

Flowers, S. (2006) *The Fraternitas Saturni* Smithsville: Runa Raven Press

Flowers, S. (1996) *Hermetic Magic* Boston:Weiser

Fries, J. (2009) *Seidways* Oxford: Mandrake

Gilbert, P. (2009) *The Compassionate Mind* London: Constable

Glucklich, A. (1997) *The End of Magic* Oxford: Oxford University Press

Hutton, R. (1995) *The Triumph of the Moon* Oxford: Oxford University Press

Hoeller, S. (2014) *The Gnostic Jung and the Seven Sermons to the Dead* Wheaton: Quest

Hoeller, S. (2002) *Gnosticism* Wheaton: Quest

Jonas, H. (1963) *The Gnostic Religion* Boston: Beacon Press

Jones, P. and Pennick, N. (1997) *A History of Pagan Europe* East Sussex: Routledge

Leadbeater, C. (1920) *The Science of the Sacraments* Los Angeles: The St. Albans Press

Levine, P. (2015) *Trauma and Memory* Berkley: North Atlantic Books

Linehan, M. (1993) *Skills Training Manual for Treating Borderline Personality Disorder* New York: The Guilford Press

Lowe,V. (1985) *Alfred North Whitehead: The Man and His Work, Volume 1: 1861-1910* Baltimore: The John Hopkins University Press

Kelly, M. (2009) *Apophis* Blurb

Mason, Barry. 'Human Systems': The Journal of Systemic Consultation &: Management. Vol. 4. 1993 pp189-200, COLFTRC & KCC

Michelet, J. (1965) *Satanism and Witchcraft* London: Tandem

Nema. (1995) *Maat Magick* Boston: Weiser

Ogilvy, G. (2006) *The Alchemist's Kitchen* Glastonbury: Wooden Books

Ouspensky, P. (1987) *In Search of the Miraculous* London: Arkana

Pagels, E.(1979) *The Gnostic Gospels* London: Weidenfield and Nicolson

Peck, M. S. (1990) *The Different Drum* London: Arrow

Pratchett, T. (2008) *Small Gods* London: Corgi

Satir, V. (1972) *Peoplemaking* Palo Alto: Science and Behaviour Books

Segal, R. (Ed.) (1995) *The Allure of Gnosticism* Chicago: Open Court

Singer, J. (2003) *A Gnostic Book of Hours* Maine: Nicolas Hays

Smith, A.P. (2008) *The Gnostics* London: Watkins Publishing

Trismegistus, H. (trans. Salaman et al 2001) *Corpus Hermeticum* London: Duckbacks

Vayne, J. and Dee, S. (2014) *Chaos Craft* Bideford: The Blog of Baphomet

Wyllie, T. (2009) *Love, Sex, Fear, Death.* Los Angeles: Feral House

Wyrd, N. and Vayne, J. (2012) *The Book of Baphomet* Oxford: Mandrake

20636490R00096

Printed in Great Britain
by Amazon